The Constitution Is My Home

The Constitution Is My Home

CONVERSATIONS ON A LIFE IN LAW

Indira Jaising

with Ritu Menon

HarperCollins *Publishers* India

First published in India by HarperCollins *Publishers* 2026
HarperCollins *Publishers* India, Cyber City,
Building 10-A, Gurugram, Haryana – 122002, India
www.harpercollins.co.in

2 4 6 8 10 9 7 5 3 1

P-ISBN: 978-93-6569-855-8
E-ISBN: 978-93-6569-785-8

Typeset in 12/16 Adobe Garamond Pro
by HarperCollins *Publishers* India Pvt. Ltd

Printed and bound at
Nutech Print Services Pvt. Ltd.

This book is printed on FSC® certified paper
which ensures responsible forest management.

*

HarperCollins *Publishers*, Macken House, 39/40 Mayor Street Upper,
Dublin 1, D01 C9W8, Ireland

I am often asked what transformation comes over me between my desk and the courtroom. I reply, preparing a case is like a pregnancy: for nine months, the idea takes shape and grows in the mind. When it is ready to be delivered, the argument is made in court. That is why I believe only a woman can argue a case well.

For my parents,
who gave me life,
and for Anand, who set me free.

CONTENTS

AUTHOR'S NOTE

Over the past six decades of my legal career, not a single day has passed without my entering a courtroom with a copy of the Constitution of India in hand. Every legal thought, every argument, every moment of clarity has been shaped by its text.

The Constitution connects it all: the case that prevented the forced eviction of pavement dwellers; the legal challenge to discriminatory service rules imposed on Air India's women employees; the long battle to establish that sexual harassment at the workplace violates the fundamental rights to equality and dignity; and countless others. It has also guided my work in the labour courts, whether defending workers' right to collective bargaining, challenging unfair dismissals or confronting the widespread misuse of contract labour.

It was the Constitution, too, that steered my shift from social and economic rights to civil and political rights, this time for more personal reasons. When you are unfairly targeted for the work you do, it is the Constitution that stands by you. I turned to it when I needed to defend myself.

I often say that the Constitution is a living companion. It does not sit in a glass case. It moves with us into courtrooms, protest sites, factories, homes and prisons. It asks us to return to its promise again and again, especially when that promise appears most under threat.

Over the years, many people I have worked with have encouraged me to write about my work. I never felt the need. I had no desire to be an academic. I preferred to remain the author of unwritten books. Instead, I found fulfilment in seeing a petitioner receive justice: a single mother gaining custody of her child; a woman securing her rightful inheritance; a judge reinstated after unfair dismissal; an elderly prisoner granted bail after being denied medical care. These moments sustained me.

Many of my colleagues went on to find their own wings and, today, some have written books of their own. They are respected human rights lawyers, mentoring younger advocates. Others who joined the struggle against domestic violence alongside me have built their own institutions and continue the work. In some ways, they are the footnotes to this book, though I imagine they would laugh at that description. We learned from one another. I still hear echoes of those conversations in courtrooms across the country.

Then there are the youngest, the law students who wait outside courtrooms or stop me in the corridors of the Supreme Court to say, 'Ma'am, I'm your fan.' I ask, 'Why?' They smile, take a selfie and disappear. Their enthusiasm always surprises me. I wonder what image of me they've encountered, perhaps one more public than personal. Still, I hold on to their words. They remind me that the paths we walk leave traces, whether we intend them to or not.

I remember one young woman in particular. I didn't know her, but after a lecture I gave, she waited outside the hall for more than an hour. When I finally stepped out, she came up to me and said, 'I just wanted to tell you, you are the reason I studied law.' I never saw her again, but that moment stayed with me. It reminded me that the labour of being a practising lawyer, of standing beside the most marginalized, had not gone unnoticed. There would be others who would follow.

This is the quiet hope that underpins this book: not that my story is unique, but that it may light the path for someone else. That, in reading about one journey, another might begin.

This book is, in essence, a conversation with Ritu Menon, whom I've known for many years and deeply respect as a writer and publisher. Its structure and scope grew out of the questions she asked. I had not planned to talk about my personal life, but Ritu insisted. 'For us women,' she said, 'the personal is the political.' She picked up on things I had said in meetings, especially about my love for the law and, slowly, the chapters began to take shape. I have always found that conversations help me think and I enjoyed the process. Before long, we had a book.

It's an unusual book, born more from dialogue than design. No chapters were mapped out in advance. There were only questions, recollections and, sometimes, laughter. This is not a memoir, nor an exhaustive account of my life's work. No life can be fully captured in words. It would be like trying to stop a river from flowing to its destination.

Readers may ask: why now? The simplest answer is that this was the moment when I had the time to enter into a sustained conversation with Ritu. But there is another reason. I wanted to look back without having to explain myself. To write honestly about what it meant to stand up, and to stay standing. This is a book about the practice of law, about what it means to argue a case in court. It is, I hope, a response to the question: Why do you practise law? But it is also about how one practises law, and for whom. That is what these conversations seek to explore.

My journey in law is not over. I still hope to work towards greater accountability from our judges and deeper fidelity to the Constitution. I was born before the Constitution came into existence. Over the past six decades, it has been my foundation and my guide. But now I also want to hold on to something else.

In 2022, the French author Annie Ernaux won the Nobel Prize for Literature. On receiving the prize, she said, 'I hope they don't steal my old age from me,' fearing the literary demands that would follow. I understand the feeling, though I do not yet feel robbed. I still have work to do, and I hope to do it.

This book has given me an opportunity I do not often allow myself: the chance to take stock of what it has meant to carve out a life in the law. That, too, has been an act of freedom.

New Delhi, 26 January 2026 **Indira Jaising**

1

SPEAKING FOR MYSELF

Ritu Menon: What have been the two most significant decisions you have taken in your life and work that were decisive at the personal level?

Indira Jaising: One of the first consequential decisions I made was not to marry. By the time I finished my law degree at twenty-two, life had unfolded with a certain ease. My only real test was academic: managing to top examinations while attending as few lectures as possible! Marriage did not so much fail to interest me as fail to appear on the horizon at all. Then, unexpectedly, it arrived as a serious proposition, and I rejected it outright.

The matter did not arise in a vacuum. My parents' concern had been gathering momentum. I was the eldest child, with two younger brothers—the elder of the two five years my junior. They were keen for him to marry, yet held fast to the belief that it was unseemly for a younger son to wed while his older sister remained unmarried. I told them plainly there was no reason for him to wait. I had no intention of marrying, and that fact need not govern his life. When he did marry, in 1967, the tension abated for the time being.

For a short while, equilibrium returned. Then my parents identified a young man they regarded suitable for me. At roughly the same time, I was diagnosed with hyperthyroidism and told that surgery would be necessary. The diagnosis did not alarm me. Hyperthyroidism carried, in those days, a faint aura of intrigue. There were whispers that hyperthyroid women were high-spirited and energetic. I found the idea oddly appealing. There was even, I thought, something faintly romantic in the admission 'I have hyperthyroidism'. I did not experience myself as ill. It felt like another turn in the course of my life, and I accepted it without fuss.

This was 1964, when understanding of treatment options was limited and rarely interrogated. The doctors decided to remove part of my thyroid gland. I did not think to question their decision; I lacked both the information and the inclination. The surgery was performed by Dr Baliga, one of Bombay's most esteemed surgeons at the time, and it proceeded without incident.

As for the young man, once he heard about my condition, his interest evaporated. The idea of marrying a 'sick' woman was, apparently, untenable. But his withdrawal did not unsettle me as much as what followed. I discovered that his family had asked my father for a dowry.

My father did not address the demand directly. Instead, he came to me and said he had commissioned some jewellery for me as part of my inheritance and saw no harm in showing it to them. I was clear. 'You can't do that. You can't give away my jewellery as dowry. I don't want it.' That was the end of it, at least for me. It was the first, and last, time my parents tried to arrange a marriage for me.

By then, my professional life was beginning to find its direction. I had joined one of Bombay's largest law firms, Mulla and Mulla—a position secured largely through my grandfather, who was a friend of the firm's founder, Nadarsha Mulla, and had persuaded him to take me on as an apprentice. My parents did not object to my working, but they preferred the stability of a firm to the uncertainties of independent practice. Then, as now, there was a clear divide between corporate lawyers and courtroom litigators. In those days, it was unusual to see women arguing cases in court. A corporate firm was considered the more appropriate setting for a woman entering the profession.

Alongside this growing engagement with professional life, my unease with dowry deepened. I had watched my cousins, just a year or two older than me, go through the ordeal. In a joint family, nothing was private. We were summoned to admire the dowry items before they were packed into trunks and dispatched to the groom's family. It revolted me. The piles of gifts were a crude advertisement of marriage as transaction. Those images stayed with me. Moreover, no one in my family questioned it. In the Sindhi community, dowry had long been customary, even though the Sind Deti Leti Act of 1939 had outlawed it well before Independence. I knew that by then. Yet the practice continued openly in my own home.

Over time, these experiences altered how I understood my own future. As my career advanced, it became central to my sense of self. I was the first woman in our family to work, and the job mattered to me in ways that went beyond occupation. It was not about money. What mattered was the fact of working—of entering a space not defined by family, of observing how people navigated their lives beyond the confines of home and of learning to navigate mine.

There were limits. Living alone was out of the question. An unmarried daughter setting up her own household would have been seen as improper, even disgraceful. I did not ask for that freedom. But within those constraints, my refusal to marry acquired a different significance.

RM: But you have nothing against the institution of marriage? This was just one incident ...

IJ: That's a hard question. As a child, I sensed that my mother was not happy in her marriage. She never said so, and we never spoke about it, but I could feel it. Later, I came to understand more. She was an only child. Her relationship with her mother was strained, but she was deeply attached to her father. An owner of cotton mills, he had been involved in the freedom movement in Sindh and gave generously to charities. He had also adopted a son, ostensibly to give her a brother, though I always suspected it had more to do with making sure his legacy and wealth passed to a male heir.

After her wedding, my mother moved to Bombay to live with my father's family. Her father died soon afterwards, while her mother and adopted brother remained in Karachi. During my early childhood, we often travelled there to visit her maternal relatives, and those visits remain among my earliest memories. During those trips, I grew close to my uncle's wife, who was also from Sindh and had been married young into the family. She later told me that as the daughter-in-law of the house she had been expected to raise her husband's sister's first child, me, and she accepted that responsibility without question. I was born before she had children of her own and it was through her, more than anyone else, I came to know many details of my early life.

My aunt told me that I had been born five years after my parents' marriage. The delay had worried my grandmother, who feared her daughter would be labelled baanjh, i.e., infertile. So, although the birth of a girl was not typically a cause for celebration, my grandmother rejoiced because my arrival had spared her daughter that cruel stigma.

Even as a child, I sensed my mother's innate sadness. She had been separated from her father and thrust into a large joint family, where she became one more daughter-in-law under the close watch of a formidable mother-in-law. Her education was cut short by marriage, but her appetite for learning remained. Since she could not step out of the house on her own, as dictated by the household rules, she found other means of widening her world. She engaged an English tutor and became fluent. The rules for the women of the household were clear: she could study at home but not cross its lakshman rekha. I watched this unfold as a child and felt a quiet anger take root.

After the Partition, when I was seven years old, my mother's maternal family arrived in Bombay as refugees. She herself never returned to Pakistan, never again saw the home where she grew up. Even back then, one could sense what that uprooting cost her, most acutely in the loss of her friends. She was permitted to meet only a few who had also resettled in Bombay, among them her closest friend from Karachi, Indira, who had become a doctor.

Every two weeks, we would visit my mother's adopted brother and his family, who had also moved to our neighbourhood. Gradually, the area took on the character of a Sindhi enclave. My father's family, by contrast, had established commercial roots in Bombay before the Partition. In time, Santa Cruz West, then a far-flung suburb, came to resemble a transplanted village, where homes and families were held together by memory and loss.

I grew up moving between my mother's and my father's joint families, absorbing their rhythms and contrasts. In my maternal family, women were encouraged to study. Two relatives close to my age went on to pursue professional careers: one became a doctor, the other a dentist.

My own views began to take shape around this time. Watching my mother's freedom shrink under the weight of custom and expectation, I came to see marriage as a structure that demanded the sacrifice of personal freedom. Uprooted from Karachi and placed in a new city and household, my mother had endured both trauma and separation. Somewhere within me, I felt that she had not truly wanted to marry but had never been given the option to refuse. I, on the other hand, had that space, and I chose not to marry.

My mother's attachment to her father remained the emotional centre of her life. From the stories she told me over the years, I came to understand what he had meant to her. He was a presence that shaped her understanding of the world. Before her marriage, she would complain to him that he did not spend enough time with her, so consumed was he by his work in the freedom movement. He would reply gently that his work called him to care for the many daughters of the nation as well.

On her wedding day, he said to her, 'You will never miss me. Wherever you turn, you will see me.' Such pithy words could hardly console a young woman about to lose the comfort of her father's daily companionship. I grew up watching her live with a quiet unhappiness, folding herself into the expectations of a joint family where authority flowed in a straight line—from grandfather to grandmother to husband.

My mother's childhood home in Karachi had pulsed with political urgency. Politics in my paternal grandfather's post-Partition household, on the other hand, was quieter. The walls were bare, save for one framed photograph of Mahatma Gandhi and Jawaharlal Nehru caught in conversation, their heads inclined towards one another in what looked like a serious exchange. That image stayed with me. In retrospect, I can see how these two men had influenced the atmosphere of the house. At times, I wonder if that influence extended even to my name and I half-suspect that, when my parents chose to name me Indira, they were thinking of Pandit Nehru's daughter.

My mother's quiet rebellion revealed itself to me gradually: in her insistence on hiring tutors, despite being forbidden to leave the house alone; in her determination to educate herself, reading whatever she could find; and in her efforts to sustain friendships with women who, like her, had migrated to Bombay from Karachi. These were things none of the other daughters-in-law—four of them living under the same roof—ever dared to do.

RM: Did you ever feel that your view could have been shaped by one individual experience rather than the institution itself?

After all, there were other marriages that seemed to work, even in your experience. Your maternal cousins worked, they were married, they became doctors, they built professional lives. Was it that your mother's experience had left such a deep impression on you or was it that you did not meet anybody you truly wanted to marry?

IJ: All the women in my mother's family who were highly educated eventually married, had children and gave up any serious pursuit of work. I, too, formed meaningful relationships with men. Some I even lived with … Yet, inevitably, the question of marriage would surface, and I would retreat. I never fully understood what went wrong. I only knew I could not bear the possessiveness that seemed to accompany it.

Slowly, I began to understand this reaction more clearly. For me, marriage signified a fundamental change in status. I later discovered that the law recognizes this as a status *in rem*. Marriage creates rights against the world: rights of inclusion and exclusion; of obligations not of one's own making but mandated by law; and expectations about founding a family and having children, often not of one's own choosing.

The men in my life knew that I worked and that I was financially independent; many even admired my commitment and achievements. Yet, they still wanted marriage, as though it were the inevitable next step. To put it plainly, marriage felt to me like a dead end, like a barrier to my own growth. I felt no attraction to the institution itself, though I had known many fulfilling relationships. My passions lay elsewhere: in law, in work, in my surroundings, in music, in life itself. But never in marriage.

Instead, I found sustenance in close friendships with women, many of whom remain dear to me to this day: Chandralekha, Asha Putli, Sarasu, Uttara ...

It was against this background I eventually decided to get married, at the age of thirty-six. Almost naturally, another decision followed: I would not have children. Though separated in time, the two choices were closely linked; one seemed to foreshadow the other. By then, I was well established as a practising lawyer.

RM: What made you believe Anand was the person you wanted to live with?

IJ: Before I answer that, I need to return to the twists and turns my life took before I turned thirty-six. While working at Mulla and Mulla, I was awarded a one-year fellowship at the Institute of Advanced Legal Studies in London, from 1969 to 1970. I was the first woman in my family to travel abroad, and my parents initially opposed the idea. They believed an unmarried daughter should not live away from home. Eventually, they relented and I left. That year proved transformative.

During this period, I also visited Paris, where I met several students who had taken part in the 1968–69 student movement in France—a massive wave of protests that began with demonstrations against university conditions and authoritarianism, then swelled into a nationwide general strike, bringing the country to the brink of revolution. Their talk of protest stirred something in me. Back in London, meanwhile, the anti-racism movement was in full swing. For me, it was not only about politics. It was the exhilaration of being present: an Indian, marching alongside Indian and Pakistani migrants against racism. It was in London that I met Suresh Grover, then part of the leadership of the anti-racism movement. I later met Anand, Suresh's elder brother, in India, when he had already decided to give up his British citizenship and migrate here.

In that setting, India's constitutional history no longer felt distant. Seeing people from undivided India protest alongside one another rendered it alive. Many of them had acquired British citizenship, while I, also of Indian origin, held Indian citizenship by birth. It was in London, too, that I first encountered law centres—walk-in spaces offering free legal advice, funded largely by local councils. I returned to Bombay the next year determined to create something similar.

Returning home, however, presented a new dilemma. I no longer wished to live with my family. But for an unmarried daughter, living alone was still unthinkable. The only way forward, it seemed, was to leave the city. Having resigned from my job before going to London, I decided to start afresh in Delhi. The romance of the Supreme Court, the centre of constitutional litigation in the country, beckoned me there.

This was 1970. I rented a small place and joined the chamber of a brilliant lawyer and member of the Communist Party of India. It was an unusual set-up, with three partners from different political parties, all fiercely intelligent. The environment was intellectually electric and deeply committed to defending workers and trade unions. The senior lawyer had argued several landmark constitutional cases and, for a time, the work felt both stimulating and politically sustaining.

Yet, despite my ideological affinity with the work, I could not stay for long. The atmosphere was thick with male chauvinism. Over the course of a year, I came to see that while the senior lawyer's politics were avowedly progressive, his worldview was unmistakably patriarchal. There was no room in that office for a woman as a professional equal. In the end, I left. That decision meant leaving the Supreme Court too, where he practised; without that professional anchor, living in Delhi no longer made sense.

My father urged me to return to Bombay. I seized the opportunity to negotiate: I would come back only if I could live independently. He agreed, perhaps reassured that he would at least see more of me than if I stayed away. And so I returned, set up my own home and began to build my practice.

Soon afterwards, I started working with K.T. Sule, a senior trade union lawyer and member of the Communist Party of India (Marxist). From him, I learned a great deal. He was already past sixty, yet he treated me as an equal from the outset. We worked closely, often laughing over briefs, and in him I found both a mentor and a colleague.

At the time, bonus disputes frequently came before the courts—they required meticulous scrutiny of company accounts since bonuses were tied to profits. Sule had an exceptional grasp of financial statements and an uncanny ability to detect how profits were concealed. Audited balance sheets were publicly available, but they often obscured more than they disclosed. He could decipher a company's inner workings through numbers alone.

Once, I asked him how he managed it. He smiled and said, 'My dear, sometimes the truth has to be stolen. After all, we represent the very people who maintain these accounts.' In time, I adopted this approach in my own practice, without guilt. It was, after all, only the truth I was stealing.

As my own practice grew, I came to represent a wide range of marginalized groups. Among them were dock workers organized by the late George Fernandes—then a leading trade unionist and socialist politician—an association that endured for many years. Later, when railway workers undertook the historic All-India Railway Workers' strike of 1974 against long-standing grievances over excessive working hours, low wages and harsh conditions, particularly for the locomotive staff, under his leadership, we represented them as well. That strike marked a turning point in Indian labour politics. It revealed both the growing strength of organized labour and the state's mounting intolerance of mass dissent, and proved to be a precursor to the declaration of the Emergency under the Indira Gandhi-led government in 1975. Fernandes himself would, in time, go on to serve as a Union minister of railways.

During this turbulent period, I had my first encounter with the Central Bureau of Investigation, the country's premier investigative agency. In May 1974, while the railway strike was underway, a group of officers arrived at my office—Room No. 6 in the old Bombay Stock Exchange building—in search of documents related to the strike.

It was then that I first heard the word 'raid': a term with no precise legal meaning, yet one capable of devastating consequences for life and liberty. The officers proceeded to seize all our files relating to the railway workers. In due course, they were returned, as they contained nothing beyond court papers already in the public domain.

With the lifting of the Emergency in 1977, our work resumed in earnest. By then, I had begun representing students expelled from various educational institutions, including St Xavier's

College in Bombay, the Film and Television Institute of India and the Indian Institute of Technology–Bombay. Such matters were treated as purely internal affairs of the universities, and student rustications were seldom entertained by the courts. There was, at the time, not even a clear legal precedent to support the complainants. Through these cases, I saw once again how easily institutions could ride roughshod over individual lives.

Around the same time, my growing interest in employment law brought me into contact with Air India air hostesses who had been denied promotion to supervisory positions. They were being treated like ornamental figures, their managerial abilities being completely ignored. The injustice was plain. It offended my sense of fairness and moved me to bring a series of constitutional challenges grounded in the right to equality.

As more such cases came our way, other left-leaning lawyers, such as Mihir Desai, Gayatri Singh, Sanobar Keshwar and Anand Grover, gravitated towards me and, together, we formed a natural alliance. Out of that shared spirit, the Lawyers Collective was born in 1980: a public-interest legal organization committed to social justice.

We were united by the conviction that the law could serve as an instrument of social and economic change, an idea shaped in part by the law centres I had encountered in London. Much of our work was undertaken pro bono, though some (mainly trade union matters) was remunerated. The organization sustained itself through a cross-subsidy model, whereby those who could afford to pay made it possible for us to represent those who could not. Around the same time, we launched *The Lawyers*, a first-of-its-kind print magazine devoted to legal and constitutional issues. It was founded on two central principles: first, to 'break the silence' created by fear of contempt proceedings and offer a space for lawyers to speak openly; and second, to explain the law in clear, accessible language to those who needed it most.

RM: What about professionally—what have been the significant decisions in your professional life?

IJ: The legal profession was, and in many ways still is, deeply shaped by networks of caste, kinship and linguistic community. As someone who did not belong to the dominant networks of the bar, I was acutely aware of these realities. I did not wish to depend on either. From early on, I knew I would have to rely entirely on my own work. There came a point in my career when moving to Delhi again became unavoidable. In December 1984, the country witnessed the Bhopal gas disaster, one of the largest industrial catastrophes in history. A lethal gas leak from the American-owned Union Carbide pesticide plant in Bhopal, Madhya Pradesh, exposed hundreds of thousands of people to methyl isocyanate, leading to immediate deaths and long-term health consequences that continue to affect survivors decades later. Soon after, I became involved in the Union Carbide case,[1] working closely with the survivors as they sought justice against a powerful multinational corporation. The litigation proceedings required a constant presence in Delhi and, as a result, I found myself constantly commuting between Bombay and the capital. The pace was relentless and impossible to sustain for long. At the same time, I was involved in the Olga Tellis case,[2] a constitutional challenge brought on behalf of pavement dwellers in Bombay who were facing mass eviction by municipal authorities. The case emerged from a sweeping drive by the Bombay Municipal

Corporation to clear what it termed 'encroachments' from public spaces. During that period, I would take the 6 a.m. flight, reach court in Delhi by 10.30 a.m. to secure a stay against eviction and return the same evening. I was perpetually in transit, with little time to recover. It was not a way of life that could endure.

I had also begun to feel that my career in Bombay had reached a plateau; if I stayed, I would simply repeat myself. You asked about the major professional decisions I have made—this was one of them.

The consequences were immediate and far-reaching. No lawyer from Bombay shifted to Delhi without a position, an assignment or a seat in Parliament; most arrived with some kind of springboard. In 1989, I moved back to Delhi without any such assurance. I found no welcoming environment at the Supreme Court. A few friends from my earlier years remained, but many were no longer in active practice. As a designated senior, joining a firm or partnership was not an option. I worked alone. Even the Lawyers' Collective could not support me financially. Somehow, the air hostesses and contract workers I had represented in Bombay continued to trust me with their cases. Their faith was my only security.

On a personal level, the move meant living apart from Anand, who wished to continue working in Bombay. When we married, we had agreed not to have children; neither of us wanted that responsibility. Anand had returned from the UK with a purpose he wanted to fulfil. He had given up his British citizenship and taken up Indian citizenship, to which he was entitled as a person of Indian origin. He did not try to dissuade me from leaving, even though it meant living separately. He told me he never wanted me to feel that he was holding back my professional growth. My decision placed a strain on our relationship, but I made it anyway. His response was generous and rare.

I had friends my age who were already married with several children, and I often wondered how they managed both family and career. Decades later, in 2014, I represented a woman judge who had been compelled to resign after an unjust transfer made it impossible for her to support her daughter's education.[3] She chose her child over her career because she had no alternative. Drawing on my own life, I argued that no woman should ever be forced to choose between her child and her profession. The court agreed. Her resignation was treated as a deemed dismissal, and she was reinstated. It remains one of the cases I'm most proud of. Professionally, it was a victory; personally, I didn't wish to confront such a situation in my own life.

I never felt the absence of children. I had grown up in a joint family, surrounded by younger children who, in many ways, felt like my own. I also knew I could not have raised a child and become the person I am today. Many successful women lawyers have had to make similar choices. I had seen, at close quarters, what marriage had done to my mother: how it narrowed her world and muted her hunger for knowledge. If I inherited anything from her, it was that hunger. Or perhaps simply the urge to be my own person.

My mother worried about my decision not to have children. Perhaps she carried the memory of a time when she had been feared to be a baanjh. Perhaps she worried about who would look after me in old age. My father, by contrast, was calm and practical. He trusted that I would find my own way.

RM: What strikes me as strange is that you came from a fairly conventional Sindhi family. Yet your non-conformism was fine as far as your father was concerned. How did that happen?

IJ: I think it had a great deal to do with his sense of authority. He was very much a patriarch when it came to my mother, his wife. With her, he exercised control. With me, he saw himself primarily as a father, not as a patriarch. Perhaps he also understood, early on, that I would not accept the restrictions applied to the other women in the family.

He supported my decision to study law without hesitation. At the time, our family was based in Bangalore for my father's work, so I completed my schooling at Bishop Cotton and my undergraduate studies at Maharani's College. After graduation, I insisted on studying law in Bombay. To make that possible, my entire family moved from Bangalore to Bombay. Even when I offered to live with relatives who were already there, he refused. An unmarried daughter, he believed, could not live without her parents. A hostel was, of course, out of the question. So, once again, he relocated the family. He knew he could not suppress my hunger for knowledge. Instead of trying to restrain me, he chose to support me.

RM: What made you decide to study law?

IJ: When I was young, we visited my maternal uncle's house every week. It overlooked the Government Law College in Bombay. Each time we went, I would watch the students gathered outside: men and women laughing, talking, moving about with an ease.

I had studied in a girls' school all my life, and the sight of men and women interacting as equals felt, to me, like a glimpse of true freedom. I decided then that one day I would be among those young women standing outside that college. Back then, I did not understand the law in any serious sense. But I understood the promise of independence it seemed to hold. Much later, I came to grasp its deeper power—not only for me, but for those I would go on to represent.

Another image from childhood stayed with me just as vividly: the night of Independence. The city of Bombay was lit up, from the Sachivalaya to Victoria Terminus and the Gateway of India. My father took me out to see the lights of freedom. That memory has never faded. Years later when I studied law, that feeling returned, this time anchored in the Constitution of India.

2

DEMOCRATIC LAWYERING

RM: Your taking up matters of workers' rights—trade unionists, air hostesses, even pavement dwellers—was this an accident or a conscious choice?

IJ: I think it had a great deal to do with the fact that I was a woman and a first-generation lawyer. I had no role models to follow. There was no template for the kind of work I wanted to do. In many ways, that was my greatest advantage. I had the freedom to shape my identity, my practice and my choices entirely on my own terms.

When I began practising, there were no collectives of lawyers working on social and economic rights. There were no NGOs in the sense we know them today, and no meaningful system of legal aid. The legal profession was dominated by traditional, family-run firms focused almost entirely on commercial law. There were individual lawyers who took up public-interest work, but there was no institutional support for the marginalized. The Lawyers' Collective emerged from the need to collectivize legal services in the public interest and make them accessible to those who needed them most.

The generation of lawyers before me was largely preoccupied with the right to property. At that time, it was still a fundamental right, though it was later removed and reintroduced as Article 300A in 1978. Much of the litigation focused on challenging land reform laws and legislation affecting business and industry. This is evident from reported judgments of the period. What is striking is that there was not a single reported judgment dealing meaningfully with the rights of marginalized communities, and virtually none addressing women's rights.

Ironically, many litigants in these cases were women. But when a land reform law was challenged in a woman's name, I often found that she was merely a proxy for her family. The litigation had little to do with her rights and everything to do with protecting family property for male heirs. In those years, women's property rights were usually asserted only after their deaths, when heirs claimed inheritance from a mother who had inherited as a widow. Most such cases were initiated by upper-caste men. Even when women approached courts on their own, they were typically upper-caste women, sometimes challenging reservations for Dalits in public employment.

There were, of course, left-wing lawyers working on civil and political rights. A formative example was the challenge to the preventive detention of comrade A.K. Gopalan, a prominent Communist leader who had been incarcerated without trial and later detained under the Preventive Detention Act of 1950. In *A.K. Gopalan vs State of Madras*, the petition questioned the legality of his continued detention. The case was argued by the

Madras-based firm V.G. Rao and Company, known for its trade union work and civil rights advocacy. There has long been a tradition of left-wing activism around civil liberties: Lawyers such as K.G. Kannabiran, for example, exposed legal impunity and so-called encounter deaths during the Emergency and successfully challenged unlawful detention as well as loss of life and liberty. Their work set important precedents for civil rights litigation. Yet, social and economic rights—housing, work, dignity, livelihood—remained largely outside the legal imagination.

This was the environment in which I set up my practice. I had no chamber to join, no senior to rely on and no established network to fall back on. I found that freedom liberating. I began with a clean slate and could decide for myself what kind of lawyer I wished to be. I chose to focus on the concerns of working women because I instinctively identified with them. Even so, this kind of litigation carried its own burden of pain, and some of it even entered my own life. In the mid-1970s, I represented an Air India air hostess who had challenged her dismissal. While her case was still pending, she died by suicide. No one can say with certainty what drove her to it. But the fact that she did not see justice in her lifetime left a lasting grief in me. It was then I realized, in a visceral way, how brutal litigation can be for ordinary people—first, in the injustice they suffer, and then in the delays, expense, absence of effective legal aid and the courts' reluctance to confront State power and corruption.

Around the same time, I began to notice a quiet deference among judges to executive authority. There was a growing belief that the government knows best what serves the nation and, therefore, ought not to be questioned. Such deference effectively amounts to an abdication of judicial responsibility and reflects a failure to enforce the Constitution. Regrettably, this tendency remains deeply embedded in Indian judicial thinking.

One historic exception was Justice H.R. Khanna's lone dissent in the additional district magistrate of Jabalpur case[1] during the Emergency in 1976, when the Supreme Court upheld the suspension of Articles 21 and 226, thereby denying citizens the right to life and liberty. Justice Khanna refused to agree. His courageous choice ultimately cost him the chief justiceship.

We are taught, as lawyers, not to take our cases personally. We are told to maintain distance, to be objective. But, in practice, that barrier often collapses. One begins to suffer with one's clients, caught alongside them in a system that drains them. Many lawyers insist such identification is unwise. Seniors and peers advise keeping a safe distance. We are expected to accept that we cannot choose our cases selectively and must learn to be 'objective' about our work.

This position is justified by invoking the 'cab rank rule', the notion that a lawyer must take the next client who approaches, just as a taxi must take the next passenger. It is defended in the name of access to justice. But that is not the same as saying everyone is entitled to our particular service. In reality, it can become a self-serving rule, serving as a convenient cover for commercial practice.

I wanted the freedom to choose. I remember arguing on behalf of pavement dwellers that, when faced with the choice between homelessness and living on the pavements of Bombay, they had a right to reside there. It was a bold claim, born out of the legal doctrine of necessity.

One of the conservative judges, Justice V.D. Tulzapurkar, who was himself from Bombay and familiar with its realities, said to me that I would be arguing the very opposite if I were representing landlords or landowners.

I replied that such a situation would not arise as I would not represent the landlords against the homeless.

He looked momentarily confused and said, 'In that case the Bar Council would take action against you.'

I told him I would welcome it. It would give me the opportunity to explain my own understanding of justice and injustice.

RM: You have often spoken about what you call 'democratic lawyering'. Could you elaborate?

IJ: Your question goes to the heart of how we understand the legitimate role of the judiciary in a democracy. As an institution, the judiciary emerged with the rise of liberalism in common-law countries and came to India through colonial rule. The idea of the rule of law has a 4,000-year history and is now accepted as the foundation of democratic governance.

In India, there was no concept of an independent judiciary in the modern sense before the Lockean idea of the social contract—a concept associated with the seventeenth-century English philosopher John Locke that recognizes individuals as rights-bearing citizens and limits the role of the state—became widely accepted. Earlier, justice was dispensed by kings or, in certain contexts, by religious authorities. Over time, courts evolved into institutions empowered to adjudicate a wide range of disputes. Judges came to bear the responsibility of balancing individual rights against executive power. Gradually, the courtroom began to reflect the aspirations of the people and their claims upon the State—social, economic and political.

The law compels individuals to take responsibility for their actions. At the same time, it obliges the State to respect the rights of citizens. Traditionally, the Left viewed law primarily as an instrument of oppression, used to discipline and control the working classes. At best, they approached courts defensively, to protect their civil and political rights and for freedom from incarceration. They did not, historically, see courts as spaces for laying down normative frameworks for social and economic rights. Litigation was not used as a tool for democratic norm-setting in these areas. There was only one important exception: the economic rights of the organized working class, particularly the right of proletarians to fair wages. This was in part because the Trade Unions Act of 1926 had already conferred legal recognition on trade unions, enabling them to register formally and represent workers in collective bargaining. The All India Trade Union Congress (AITUC), established in 1920 as one of the country's earliest national trade union federations, provided an organizational platform for labour activism. After Independence, most political parties developed affiliated trade unions of their own. These unions, in turn, had their own network of specialized labour lawyers. In that sense, the organized working class was relatively well represented in the courts. Yet these trade union lawyers rarely ventured into other areas of social justice. More broadly, left-wing lawyers tended to use the Constitution as a shield rather than a sword. They relied on it to defend rights, not to expand them.

Lawyers such as R.K. Garg and M.K. Ramamurthy regularly represented working-class interests before the Supreme Court.

They were deeply committed constitutionalists, active in the defence of civil and political freedoms. But even they did not decisively enter the terrain of social and economic rights as a field for judicial norm-setting. Nor did they see courts as a legitimate forum for democratic discourse. It is in that gap between constitutional promise and lived reality that democratic lawyering, as I understand it, begins.

Here I parted company with the generation before me, who, often out of historical and political necessity, restricted their courtroom work to defending civil and political rights rather than advancing economic and social ones.

I could not accept that limitation. In my own practice, I began to see how constitutional law could be mobilized to enforce substantive rights. It was the guarantee of non-discrimination, prohibiting unequal treatment on grounds such as sex, that brought relief to the air hostesses whose case I argued. Few left-wing lawyers at the time recognized the power of constitutional litigation in the field of social and economic rights.

So, when I established my own practice, it was natural for me to work alongside the trade union movement. But I also chose to widen the frame: to take up women's rights and broader questions of social and economic justice. I began to pursue cases that treated livelihood, dignity and access to public space as constitutional concerns flowing from the guarantees of equality, freedom and the right to life itself.

I fully understood the force of this approach when I took up the hawkers' case in the early 1980s. It was the post-Emergency period, when the higher judiciary had begun to cautiously reinvent itself. Public interest litigation, an innovation of the Supreme Court that relaxed rules of standing to allow public-spirited individuals to approach the court on behalf of disadvantaged groups, had started to open the judicial process to the marginalized. Even so, access to justice remained deeply uneven. At the time, the Bombay Municipal Corporation had issued barely 14,000 hawking licences in a metropolis with several lakh street vendors. This imbalance inevitably bred corruption. Unlicensed vendors were forced to pay regular bribes to the police to continue earning a living. It was George Fernandes who first grasped the scale of the problem. He organized the vendors and brought their struggle to me. By then, many had begun turning to the Bombay underworld to mediate disputes with the police. The legal system barely figured in their lives.

When George approached me, I decided to take the matter to court. No one had attempted this before. A hawking licence was treated as a discretionary favour rather than an incident of the constitutional right to practise a trade and carry on a livelihood. Yet hawkers performed an indispensable function in Bombay's working-class economy. Around Victoria Terminus—now renamed Chhatrapati Shivaji Maharaj Terminus—they sold affordable vegetables, fruits and daily essentials to women rushing to catch fast trains home. These commuters depended on street vendors to save precious time and manage their households. In many respects, South Bombay functioned on the twin pillars of its local train network and its informal street economy. Food vendors, too, sustained a large lunchtime population, providing meals at prices wage-earners could afford.

The principal argument deployed against hawkers was that they were a 'nuisance' to pedestrians. Food vendors faced an even harsher charge: that their wares were unhygienic and a threat to public health. We decided to test this claim empirically.

We bought a glass of orange juice from a five-star hotel and sent it to Dr Amin's Laboratory in South Bombay—an accredited facility for chemical and bacteriological analysis. As expected, the hotel juice was also found to be contaminated with bacteria. Armed with this report, we moved the high court seeking the restoration of the vendors' licences. The BMC, and the hotel, soon found themselves the subject of public ridicule, both in the courtroom and in the media. The court ultimately directed that designated food courts be constructed, equipped with clean water and proper waste-disposal facilities. But beyond establishing the public value of the vendors, we also raised the issue of systemic corruption in the police force. We did not deny that bribes had been paid. Many warned me that it was dangerous to admit this. Yet it was simply the truth. Hawkers paid the police regularly, often through intermediaries linked to the underworld, in order to survive. It was only when the court realized that the BMC was losing substantial revenue to this shadow economy of bribery that the matter took a decisive turn. The litigation culminated in what came to be known as the Bombay Hawkers' Union case[2], one of the earliest matters before the Supreme Court to recognize livelihood and street trading as questions of social and economic rights under the Constitution.

RM: This case conceptualized denial of the right to work as an infringement of the fundamental right to life and liberty. Can you say more about that?

IJ: Yes. That was the crucial shift in how hawking was understood. Street vendors were no longer seen as illegal encroachers or temporary nuisances. They were recognized as workers entitled to dignity, protection and constitutional rights, just like the shopkeepers who lined Bombay's streets. The struggle was for that recognition. In 1984, the Bombay Hawkers' Union challenged the constitutional validity of Sections 313, 313A, 314(3) and 497 of the Bombay Municipal Corporation Act, 1888. These provisions empowered the BMC to deny or renew hawking licences and to seize goods without giving hawkers any opportunity to be heard. In effect, a person's livelihood could be taken away overnight, without explanation or remedy.

The union contended that the hawkers had a fundamental right to carry on their trade, business or occupation, and that the arbitrary denials of licences, which rendered them liable to be removed along with their goods, unlawfully interfered with this right. When licences were refused, vendors were removed from the streets and thereby deprived of their means of survival.

During the proceedings, following the intervention of the court, the BMC formulated a city-wide licensing scheme, creating designated 'hawking zones'. When the court examined the merits of the scheme, two conditions stood out. The first prohibited the sale of cooked food, cut fruits and similar items. The second restricted hawking hours to between 7 a.m. and 9 p.m.

The first condition was struck down as an 'unreasonable restriction' on the hawkers' right to trade or business. The bench noted that thousands of working families relied on affordable food sold by street vendors. Preventing hawkers from selling cooked food and fresh produce would harm precisely those whom the law was meant to protect. The second restriction was modified. Hawking hours were extended until 10.00 p.m., with the court wryly observing that the 'nights are quite young at 10 p.m.' in Bombay.

On the issue of hawking and non-hawking zones, the court directed the municipal commissioner to adopt certain modalities. Licences could not be arbitrarily refused in designated zones, except for good reason. Any discretion exercised by the municipal commissioner had to be reasonable, transparent and in the public interest. The corporation was required to consult stakeholders and involve hawkers in decisions affecting their livelihoods. The bench laid down an important precedent: hawkers had a constitutional right to earn a living on public streets, subject to fair regulation by the BMC. The judgment also empowered hawkers to have a say in any future alterations to the scheme regulating their trade.

I still remember one image from that case. A woman selling bananas on the pavement had been kicked by a police officer. Her basket—her only source of income—was crushed under his boots. I placed a photograph depicting the scene before the judges to convey the reality behind the legal arguments.

K.K. Venugopal, who was appearing for the BMC, remarked, 'There can be no argument against a photograph.' We won the case. For the first time in Indian legal history, the court held that hawkers had a right to vend and directed the corporation to demarcate hawking zones. Over time, licences were issued. The grip of the underworld over street vending weakened. A parallel economy based on extortion began to collapse.

For me, the case marked a turning point. It revealed the power of the law to defend the economic rights of the self-employed and those with no other means of survival aside from their labour. These propertyless people emerged as the new claimants in constitutional litigation. From then on, I never hesitated to approach the courts to argue for substantive justice on their behalf. Decades later, this trajectory contributed to broader movements for vendors' rights, culminating in the Street Vendors (Protection of Livelihood and Regulation of Street Vending) Act, 2014, which recognized livelihood and social security as statutory entitlements.

I have always believed that workers have little to lose by turning to the courts. They have no access to political power. They cannot lobby legislators. They are not part of elite networks. They do not meet judges socially. They cannot afford bribes. All they have is the Constitution.

It gives them the right to carry on their trade like anyone else. It is both their shield and their source of power. And the courtroom is the space where that power can be asserted.

I adopted the same approach in the subsequent pavement dwellers' case, *Olga Tellis vs Bombay Municipal Corporation* in 1985.[3] When A.R. Antulay was the chief minister of Maharashtra, his government sought to remove pavement dwellers from the city. People were rounded up, packed into buses and dropped at the borders of the state. The operation was carried out under provisions of the BMC act that permitted the removal of 'boxes and benches' from pavements.

I was appalled by this equation of human beings with inanimate objects. Boxes and benches have no right to notice or contest their removal. They have no right to be heard. Under this interpretation, municipal authorities could descend on entire communities and remove them like refuse.

While the Bombay High Court granted temporary relief during the monsoon, Olga Tellis, a journalist, challenged the mass eviction in the Supreme Court in 1985. I appeared on her behalf. Once again, I invoked the power of a constitutional court, arguing that this action went against the right to life and liberty, including the right to a livelihood, under Article 21. These migrants had come to Bombay to earn a living; evicting them without the provision of alternative housing or livelihoods was a violation of their fundamental rights. The court accepted this argument in a history-making case that sparked a nation-wide movement for housing rights and, ultimately, led to legislation for low-income housing in cities like Bombay.

In its landmark judgment the Supreme Court gave substantive meaning and depth to the phrase 'right to life' under Article 21 of the Constitution. The case challenged the forcible eviction of pavement dwellers and the demolition of their shelters under Section 314 of the Bombay Municipal Corporation Act, on the grounds that such action violated their right to livelihood under Articles 19 (freedom of occupation) and 21.

Although the bench ultimately upheld the power of eviction, it did so subject to important conditions. It recorded the State's assurance that alternative sites would be provided. It directed that rehabilitation policies be pursued in earnest. It prohibited evictions during the monsoon, recognizing how it rendered the homeless particularly vulnerable. The true significance of this decision lies in its constitutional reasoning. In a historic first, the Supreme Court articulated livelihood as an integral component of the right to life.

The opening passages of Chief Justice Y.V. Chandrachud's judgment capture this shift. They recognize distress migration from rural areas as a consequence of economic necessity and locate responsibility for housing and rehabilitation squarely with the State. It reads:

These Writ Petitions portray the plight of lakhs of persons who live on pavements and in slums in the city of Bombay. They constitute nearly half the population of the city. The first group of petitions relates to pavement dwellers while the second group relates to both pavement and Basti or Slum dwellers. Those who have made pavements their homes exist in the midst of filth and squalor, which has to be seen to believed. Rabid dogs in search of stinking meat and cats in search of hungry rats keep them company. They cook and sleep where they ease, for no conveniences are available to them. Their daughters, come of age, bathe under the nosy gaze of passers by, unmindful of the feminine sense of bashfulness ...

It is these men and women who have come to this Court to ask for a judgment that they cannot be evicted from their squalid shelters without being offered alternative accommodation. They rely for their rights on Article 21 of the Constitution which guarantees that no person shall be deprived of their life except according to procedure established by law. They do not contend that they have a right to live on the pavements—their contention is that they have a right *to live*, a right which cannot be exercised without the means of livelihood. They have no option but to flock to big cities like Bombay, which provide the means for bare subsistence. They only choose a pavement or a slum which is nearest to their place of work. In a word, their plea is that the right to life is illusory without a right to the protection of the means by which alone life can be lived. And the right to life can only be taken away or abridged by a procedure established by law, which has to

> be fair and reasonable, not fanciful or arbitrary, such as is prescribed by the Bombay Municipal Corporation Act or the Bombay Police Act. They also rely upon their right to reside and settle in any part of the country which is guaranteed by Article 19(1)(e).[emphasis mine][4]

The bench held that an essential component of the right to life is the right to livelihood. To deprive a person of their means of earning is, in effect, to deprive them of life itself. The court recognized that rural-to-urban migration in India is driven largely by economic compulsion. People do not move to cities from the hinterlands by choice. In that context, the right to livelihood assumes particular constitutional importance. Another key aspect of the judgment was its insistence that the fundamental rights under Part III of the Constitution and the Directive Principles of State Policy cannot operate in isolation. The directive principles envision a social order in which all citizens have adequate means of livelihood. The court directed that the fundamental rights and these principles must be read together if the constitutional rights are to be given real meaning.

The Supreme Court also recognized that pavement dwellers occupy public spaces out of sheer helplessness rather than any criminal intent. It rejected the BMC's plea that no prior notice was required before eviction because such notice would serve no purpose. The court observed that this view betrayed a misunderstanding of the right to be heard before suffering adverse consequences, an important principle of natural justice. It equated eviction from the pavement with the destruction of a home.

Some of the court's observations conveyed what eviction means for those who live on the margins:

> Eviction of the pavement or slum dweller not only means his removal from the house but the destruction of the house itself. And the destruction of a dwelling house is the end of all that one holds dear in life. Humbler the dwelling, greater the suffering and more intense the sense of loss.

The central theme of the Olga Tellis judgment is its recognition that poverty itself can become a barrier to the realization of fundamental rights. The court acknowledged the systemic forces of impoverishment that force people to migrate to cities and live in squalor simply to eke out a living. It also affirmed the need to protect the dignity of such persons, recognizing dignity as an inextricable part of the right to life.

The case continues to have a lasting influence. It has shaped judicial opinion on the right to housing and on the legality of evictions in the context of urban migration. Equally significant is its enunciation of the right to livelihood as a facet of the right to life. It remains a guiding precedent in the Supreme Court to this day.

RM: In a related case, you represented Ela R. Bhatt and the Self-Employed Women's Association in a case regarding women vegetable vendors, didn't you?

IJ: Yes. I argued what came to be known as the Manek Chowk case in the Supreme Court in in the 1980s.[5] This case centred on women vegetable vendors who had long earned their livelihood at Manek Chowk, a public square in Ahmedabad, Gujarat. Long before the city encroached and transformed the area into a congested traffic hub, these women had been vending there. In 1982, when the municipal corporation decided to clear the space for infrastructure development, it ordered their eviction. The women, members of the Self-Employed Women's Association (SEWA), refused to leave.

For years, I had grappled with a deceptively simple question: how does one organize the self-employed? My understanding of trade unionism, which was shaped by the legal architecture of the Trade Unions Act, excluded them entirely and assumed unions were exclusively for industrial workers. The act, then and now, is premised on the binary of the employer and employee. By definition, employment presupposes the existence of an employer, a wage structure and, therefore, the possibility of organizing for fairer conditions.

It was Ela Bhatt, the visionary founder of SEWA and a trade unionist, who changed my thinking. She introduced me to the idea that the self-employed could and must be organized to claim their rights. Even then, I pressed the question: who are the self-employed to bargain with? Against whom do they raise their demands?

Answers emerged from my experience as the counsel in the Bombay Hawkers' Union case. Around the same time, the connection between my work for the hawkers, led by George Fernandes, and SEWA, led by Ela Bhatt, became unmistakable. SEWA approached me after its members were being criminally prosecuted for street vending without licences. Their handcarts and goods were seized, and fines were imposed for the release of their goods and carts. Ironically, these fine receipts, which had been diligently preserved by the women, later became crucial evidence. They evidenced how long the women had engaged in street vending as well as the state's tacit acknowledgment of their activity over time.

It was through this case that I found my answer: the self-employed can be unionized by trade unionists who carry with them the knowledge, experience and strategies of organizing formal-sector workers. Neither Fernandes nor Bhatt could have mobilized the self-employed without their grounding in the organized labour movement.

Bhatt herself was no stranger to the ethos of Gandhian labour politics. Before founding SEWA, she had worked with the Ahmedabad Textile Labour Association, closely associated with M.K. Gandhi. Under her visionary leadership, SEWA developed the concept of the natural market, i.e., spaces that organically evolved as centres of commerce, serving the everyday needs of urban consumers. Manek Chowk embodied this idea: the women vendors had operated there for decades in what is now the heart of the city. When the corporation attempted to displace them in the name of traffic management and road widening, SEWA resisted.

A cluster of more than a hundred women sold vegetables there, their families entirely dependent on these earnings. They now faced imminent eviction. SEWA argued that these women had occupied this natural market long before the city grew around it, and they had a prior right to stay. They were also meeting an obvious consumer need, catering to busy commuters grabbing vegetables on their way home.

I appeared on behalf of SEWA before a Supreme Court bench presided over by Justice P.N. Bhagwati. The court ruled that the women could not be evicted unless they were accommodated in a newly constructed municipal market at the same location. It was a landmark ruling. We celebrated with baskets of fruits and vegetables, handed to us by the very women whose lives we had defended.

Ela Bhatt pressed forward. She lobbied relentlessly for legislation that would protect the rights of hawkers. The initiatives that began in Ahmedabad and Bombay crystallized into a national movement. Today, every state has a hawkers' union under the umbrella of the National Hawker Federation. The culmination of this struggle was the passage of the Street Vendors (Protection of Livelihood and Regulation of Street Vending) Act, 2014, by the United Progressive Alliance government. Bhatt's decades-long demand for state recognition of the informal economy had finally become law.

Ela was jubilant. SEWA marked the occasion with celebration: women wove garlands of vegetables for her and for me. I remember her saying, 'I never thought I would see this day before I died.' Yet, even this recognition did not come easily. SEWA was later denied trade union status and excluded from the Indian Labour Conference, a tripartite forum of government, employers and workers meant to shape national labour policy. Once again, we turned to the courts. I argued SEWA's case before the Delhi High Court. We won. SEWA was recognized as a trade union, securing a seat at the policy-making table for the self-employed.

This, then, is what the law must do: transform the abstract guarantees of the Constitution into material rights for the marginalized. My colleagues and I set out to use it to secure social and economic entitlements, particularly the fundamental right to trade and carry on business, a domain until then monopolized by corporate houses.

There's long been a debate among activists and jurists about whether the law is a legitimate site for resolving conflict or articulating social demands and about its legitimate place as an instrument of social change. I have always believed that the law is a legitimate instrument for social change. Others argue that rights must be fought for and defended on the streets through struggle and advocacy rather than in courtrooms. It need not be an either-or choice. Instead it should be a strategic choice, shaped by context.

The modern, legitimate use of civil society mobilization began under colonial rule, when Gandhi launched civil disobedience movements and mass protests against the British. At that time, there was no meaningful recourse to judicial review of executive action. Freedom fighters, therefore, turned to non-cooperation and the withdrawal of consent from colonial institutions as legitimate means of demanding an end to foreign rule. Justice, in those circumstances, required direct confrontation with the powers that be. Gandhi maintained that when all lawful avenues are exhausted, civil disobedience becomes a duty. This principle still holds true.

But there is a difference. Dr B.R. Ambedkar pointed to this distinction. He argued that once a Constitution is in place, social struggles must, as far as possible, be channelled through courts, elections and legislatures.[6] Today, constitutional courts exist precisely to advance these goals of social and economic justice. Courts are not antithetical to struggle. Rather, they are one of its institutional forms. The history of our republic reveals both the potential and the limits of legal routes to justice. Litigation and mobilization should be seen as complementary, not mutually exclusive, paths.

The Gandhian right to protest retains its primacy in our discourse of rights. Protest is not the opposite of legal strategy. It is often what gives it moral force. Still, there is some legitimate concern about the overuse and un-strategic use of judicial review by civil society actors. Excessive reliance on courts can lead to the depoliticization of movements and a dilution of their collective moral power. Courts may set normative standards, but they cannot substitute for political action and grassroots organization.

This is what I mean by 'democratic lawyering'. There is a long-standing symbiotic relationship between lawyers and social movements that predates the Constitution. The de facto birth of rights has often led to their de jure recognition. Experience teaches us that civil and political rights cannot be disentangled from social and economic rights. Each sustains the other. That insight has shaped my own role as a lawyer. I often say that the law is like plasticine. It is not hewn in stone. Democratic lawyering involves shaping that clay and converting the gains of collective struggle into legal entitlements.

There have been both successes and failures. Even unsuccessful cases have, at times, led to legislative reform. The Indian legal system allows for judicial correction through legislative amendment, as occurred after the Emergency. The Janata Dal government amended the Constitution to ensure that the right to life and personal liberty could never again be suspended. Political change enabled legal correction, underscoring the dynamic relationship between courts and democratic politics.

As I will discuss later, my own experience of victimization taught me that the right to speak up is the foundation of all meaningful change. It is that very right that is under attack in the country today.

It is my faith in the democratic process that led me to treat the Supreme Court as a forum for justice. Before our efforts, such a strategy was largely neglected. The moment was opportune: in the aftermath of the Emergency, the court was chastened by its own failures and seemed willing to reimagine its role. Access to justice was liberalized, creating the conditions for a series of landmark cases, including those arising out of the Asiad construction projects in Delhi. *In People's Union for Democratic Rights vs Union of India* (1982), popularly known as the Asiad Workers' Case, the Supreme Court entertained a petition brought by the People's Union for Democratic Rights, a civil liberties organization. The apex court examined evidence that labourers employed in the Asian Games construction works, many of them migrants from impoverished rural regions, were being paid below the statutory minimum wage and subjected to exploitative conditions. The court held that the right to life under Article 21 included the right to live with basic human dignity, and ruled that the payment of wages below the legal minimum amounted to forced labour under Article 23, since economic necessity could operate as a form of coercion. The judgment effectively transformed constitutional guarantees into enforceable protections. Over time, this strategy came to be known as public interest ligation. In my opinion, it has been one of the most effective tools for decolonizing India's legal system, which was designed to preserve order and protect property.

Justice P.N. Bhagwati, the key architect of this litigation model, argued that the traditional British adversarial system was ill-suited to the Indian context. It presumed a citizen who could identify a legal wrong and seek redress on their own. In a country marked by widespread illiteracy and economic deprivation, most citizens had no access to this form of justice. To address this inequity, *locus standi*—the rule determining who has the standing to file a case—was loosened. Public-spirited individuals and organizations were permitted to move the court on behalf of those unable to do so themselves.

Swami Agnivesh, a prominent social reformer and Arya Samaj leader, for example, brought transformative litigation for bonded labourers who were trapped in conditions of debt servitude that persisted despite statutory abolition.

As time has gone by, the character of public interest litigation evolved. An effort to secure the rights of the marginalized gradually expanded into broader questions of economic and social justice. More recently, courts have attempted to grapple with environmental degradation and ecological protection. But these attempts have often failed, as they require the judiciary to confront entrenched corporate interests prevailing under the guise of 'development', a term so hollowed out it now blinds judicial reasoning.

Efforts to hold monopolistic business houses accountable, or to examine their ties to ruling parties, are routinely met with a counter-narrative that casts judges as overreaching into the domain of policy. That narrative is often orchestrated by the executive. Justice Bhagwati's early description of PIL as 'non-adversarial'—meaning, the court, the petitioner and the State were to collaborate in pursuit of justice rather than contest one another as traditional opponents—no longer holds. What is worse, judges now frequently initiate suo motu proceedings, in which courts initiate action on their own motion, sometimes on the basis of newspaper reports. This risks turning judicial review on its head. Where, then, is the line between the aggrieved and the adjudicator? Injury is no longer self-perceived; it is judicially perceived. That shift carries danger. Judiciary reasoning may then be guided by personal prejudice or political ideology rather than the Constitution.

There have also been objections to the very term 'public interest litigation'. Scholars such as Upendra Baxi have preferred the 'social action litigation', highlighting the primacy of social activism.[7] But that framing, in my view, risks underutilizing the independent force of constitutional mechanisms and, at times, ironically places too much faith in the State to respond to social activism. In recent years, PIL has attracted searing criticism. To me, it appears to have become progressively more judge-directed. The tendency to rely on Articles 14, 19 and 21, together with Article 142, as constitutional remedies for every problem has weakened interpretive skills and narrowed constitutional vision. In cases concerning social and economic rights, the Supreme Court has often been technical and restrictive. But in matters of personal liberty, where fidelity to law and procedure ought to be exacting, it has often adopted a more liberal approach to the requirement of procedure established by law.

The aftermath of the Bhopal gas disaster in the 1980s provides a striking illustration of the tensions that arise when the State assumes exclusive authority to represent victims of mass harm. Despite the involvement of numerous activists and academics, few challenged the constitutional validity of the Bhopal Gas Leak Disaster (Processing of Claims) Act, 1985. The statute granted the Government of India exclusive authority to litigate in a parens patriae capacity, on behalf of the victims. It rested on a flawed assumption that the victims were too scattered and vulnerable to pursue their claims independently. The consequence was that the State negotiated a settlement with the Union Carbide

Corporation that was widely regarded as both legally inadequate and morally indefensible.

It was the journalist Raj Kumar Keswani who had anticipated the scale of the disaster and questioned the law that stripped victims of their agency. Before the tragedy, Keswani had published three articles warning of the dangers posed by the Union Carbide plant in Bhopal. I filed a petition on his behalf in the Supreme Court, challenging the government's monopoly over the litigation. Little attention was paid at the time to the Indian government's clear conflict of interest. Through the Life Insurance Corporation of India, a state-owned insurer, the Government of India held shares in Union Carbide India Ltd (UCIL), the subsidiary that operated the plant. That financial stake alone should have disqualified the State from acting as the sole litigant. While it was crucial to establish multinational liability and hold Union Carbide Corporation (UCC) accountable, it was equally necessary to scrutinize the Indian government's own regulatory failure. That failure enabled a toxic chemical industry to function without adequate oversight.

Yet the government's shareholding in UCIL was never raised before any court. The decision to vest exclusive authority in the Union of India and to exclude the victims themselves from the litigation proved calamitous. It resulted in a settlement that was unconscionably low and, even decades later, the question of just compensation remains unsettled. The only tangible legal outcome of the disaster was the passage of the Environment (Protection) Act, 1986, which consolidated and expanded the central government's powers to regulate industrial activity and safeguard the environment. But even this legacy is rarely associated, in the public mind, with the suffering of the people of

Bhopal. It ought to be. That law stands, in a sense, as their final and largely unacknowledged gift to the nation.

Whatever one's preferred route to the constitutional court, there has always been a current of resistance, whether in the domain of civil and political rights or in that of social and economic rights, against the repressive power of the State. Democratic lawyering must, therefore, also serve as a dual function: as a shield against authoritarianism as well as a vehicle for social and economic transformation.

RM: Specifically regarding women, other than those in formal or self-employment, what has been your experience in court?

IJ: Another branch of law I practised was matrimonial and divorce litigation. In each of these cases, I found myself representing the woman, never the husband. The women came, often as a last resort, and the system they encountered was indifferent, sometimes hostile. One of the cases I handled was that of the lawyer Flavia Agnes, who later became a prominent advocate for women's rights. At the time, there were no shelters for women fleeing domestic violence. Agnes, along with her children, took shelter in my home. She had fled a violent marriage and turned to the courts for protection. Repeatedly, the courts tried to press her back into the marriage, treating her suffering as destiny. The case helped me recognize domestic violence as a systemic injustice, whereby the judiciary's typical response was deference to male authority and the marital status quo. Over time, many more women came to me with similar stories.

As I continued this work, cases involving another disturbing form of abuse came to me: child sexual abuse within the family, particularly those perpetrated by fathers. One encounter remains seared in my memory. A woman from a wealthy Marwari joint family came seeking a divorce. She had three young daughters. When I asked her to articulate her grounds, she couldn't bring herself to say clearly that her husband was abusing their children. She sat before me, her eyes teary and devoid of hope. Her brothers accompanied her and remained in the room throughout, their presence ensuring her silence. She did not feel safe confiding in me with them present. I tried to assure her she could be helped, and that protection was possible, but she never came back. I often wonder what became of her and of those girls.

That case confirmed for me that wealth is no shield against domestic violence. I have handled divorce cases of women married into rich and powerful families, whose privilege offered them neither protection from violence nor from being thrown out of their homes. One woman, in a remarkable act of courage, decided to publicly expose the hypocrisy of the family that had cast her out. She pitched a tent outside her matrimonial home in an elite locality and refused to leave until the family acknowledged her and settled her claims.

The experiences I gathered while representing such women in the late 1970s and early 1980s eventually informed my role in conceptualizing and drafting the law on domestic violence between 1998 and 2005.[8] Previously, women had no remedy against domestic violence except divorce, which many did not want or could afford. Even today, India has no law granting joint ownership of matrimonial property. A wife may be turned out the marital home empty-handed, without any proprietorial claim. She must suffer the violence, or vanish from it. Domestic violence in India has a grim specificity. A woman is rendered homeless by being physically expelled. Or she is driven to walk out herself under untolerable conditions. I have often said a woman is less protected in her matrimonial home than a tenant. Her only social security is her natal family. Yet many families refuse to take the women back, telling her once she marries, only her dead body will leave her husband's house. Sadly, for victims of domestic violence, this is often true.

In the early 1980s, Satyarani Chadha became one of the first mothers to publicly contest the recording of her daughter's death in the matrimonial home as an 'accident'. She challenged the police decision to close her complaint against her son-in-law for murder. Her daughter, burned alive, was said to have died when a kerosene stove burst and her sari caught fire. Such stories became grimly familiar, used to explain away what became euphemistically known as stove burst deaths.

Despite laws against cruelty to women, their suffering rarely draws serious attention until they are dead. In an article in the *Economic and Political Weekly* in 2014, I called this phenomenon 'Concern for the Dead, Condemnation for the Living'.[9]

I once watched a priest-undertaker prepare the body of a young married woman for cremation. The corpse was draped in a red sari. The priest performed his rites with solemn devotion. It struck me then that these women are often accorded more tenderness in death than they were permitted in life. The psychology of domestic violence is complex, shaped by fear and social conditioning.

I have known women who returned to their natal homes to escape domestic violence, only to be sent back and later discovered dead. A surgeon friend once described her days in medical training, where she saw women with fatal injuries who refused to implicate their husbands as perpetrators, fearing retaliation should they survive. My experiences in the United States offered a contrast. There, women fleeing abuse could seek refuge in shelters, sometimes under assumed names. Not all were safe, of course; some were hunted down and killed by their abusers. But there existed, at least, institutional recognition of a woman's right to escape. In India, I see far fewer such structures of support. Here, natal families frequently disclaim responsibility for married daughters, leaving them with nowhere to go.

RM: Do you see a conceptual distinction between democratic lawyering and feminist lawyering, or is it just a question of emphasis?

IJ: I do see a distinction. My work in women's rights has led me to conclude that the constitutional promises of equality before the law and equal protection under it often offer little to women. While the Constitution guarantees equality, this right holds scant meaning for those who begin from unequal positions. In some cases, it may even reinforce existing disparities. The US Constitution, for example, enshrined equality as a principle, yet simultaneously upheld slavery as a legal institution.

Democratic lawyering advances the ideals of liberalism. It draws strength from the vision of the welfare state outlined in the Directive Principles of State Policy. When I speak of democratic lawyering, I refer to the effort to expand the Constitution's liberal foundations and to realize its commitment to social justice through welfare-based governance.

Feminist lawyering, however, begins from a different premise. It accepts that men and women do not occupy equal footing, and that the liberal notion of equality between equals is, therefore, structurally inadequate. When legal equality is applied uniformly, it often conceals injustice rather than addressing it. It creates the illusion of fairness while overlooking deep-rooted disadvantage sustained by patriarchal norms and institutional bias. Our Constitution already acknowledges such hierarchies in the context of caste and addresses them through provisions such as reservations in public employment. These measures have been routinely contested on the grounds that they violate equality for the privileged classes. Nonetheless, the courts have consistently upheld them, affirming the concept of substantive equality i.e., a justice that accounts for structural disadvantage and seeks to correct its consequences, not merely its surface appearance.

This line of reasoning made it easier to extend such logic to gender-based inequalities. I have long questioned why the Constitution-makers did not include similar provisions for women, given their historical exclusion from public life. While horizontal quotas now exist for women within the Scheduled Castes and Scheduled Tribes categories, the absence of broader constitutional backing means gender-based measures remain vulnerable to challenge in the name of neutrality. Still, the constitutional landscape was not hostile to such claims. It was already evolving towards an understanding of inequality as a product of enduring hierarchies rather than isolated acts of exclusion.

For over forty years, the women's movement in India has demanded political representation. The Constitution (106th Amendment) Act, 2023, reflects this demand by reserving one-third of seats for women in the Lok Sabha and state assemblies. But implementation has been postponed until a future delimitation based on a census that remains overdue since 2011.

These legal and philosophical developments found fuller expression in both feminist and anti-caste thought. In 1989, the American legal scholar Catharine A. MacKinnon published *Towards a Feminist Theory of the State*, arguing that meaningful equality for women could not be achieved without breaking down the hierarchies embedded in law and society. More than half a century earlier, Dr B.R. Ambedkar had offered a parallel diagnosis of caste. He exposed Hinduism's 'ascending order of reverence and descending order of contempt' and identified its endurance in the practice of endogamy.[10]

The resonance is striking. MacKinnon's insistence—formulated in a different context and era—that hierarchical power structures must be dismantled for substantive equality mirrors Dr Ambedkar's earlier call to eradicate caste-based structures. Because I had engaged deeply with Ambedkar's writings and relied on them extensively in defending caste-based reservations, these similarities informed my feminist legal practice in immediate and lasting ways.

The Indian judiciary, too, had already begun to recognize the Constitution's transformative potential. Reservation was increasingly viewed as a legitimate mechanism to genuine equality. Ambedkar's insights into endogamy foreshadowed what we now describe as intersectionality.

From this vantage, it became possible to introduce the principle of substantive equality into arguments for women's rights. Dismantling gendered hierarchy, rather than merely invoking formal parity, became the only effective way to assert women's claims.

RM: If liberalism, which underpins democratic lawyering, is not the answer, then where do we look?

IJ: I've already answered the question. When it comes to equality, there is no clarity on what this right meaningfully offers women—socially, economically and politically. Since the rule of law became a governing principle, equality has been interpreted as equality *among equals*. This is precisely what enabled the US to reconcile slavery with the rule of law. A similar distortion threatens women in India, for whom the guarantee of equality before the law may ultimately carry little substance.

Jurists have begun to speak of substantive equality. I prefer to understand it as the morality of the Constitution, as articulated in the Preamble. The division between law and morality has always troubled me. Transformative constitutionalism, developed in South Africa and now part of Indian legal discourse, seeks to bridge this divide by interpreting the Constitution as a tool of social change. But that bridge can only truly hold if it rests on a coherent theory of justice rooted in substantive equality. The idea of equality in outcomes has yet to be fully incorporated into our constitutional thinking.

The Directive Principles of State Policy outline a vision of distributive justice through equitable distribution of resources and opportunities. Thinkers such as Amartya Sen and Martha Nussbaum have expanded this further through the capabilities approach, which measures justice by what individuals are truly able to do and become. It aims to give a practical meaning to distributive justice. However, neither the directive principles nor the capabilities framework addresses the deeper hierarchies of caste, gender and religion.

That is why these issues cannot be addressed through equality alone. The law cannot simply be applied *equally* in these contexts. It is not enough to argue that preventing a married woman from filing a complaint of rape against her husband amounts to discrimination between married and unmarried women. It is essential to recognize that marital rape stems from the imbalance of power within marriage and the family, and that this structure itself must be critically examined.

I have argued that the institution of marriage itself needs to be redefined before the marital rape exception can be meaningfully eliminated. It may surprise you to know that our laws provide no real definition of marriage. The law tells us how to enter a marriage and how to exit it. But it does not explain what marriage *is*. Until we define it as a relationship founded on mutual care, affection and shared responsibility, including respect for the sexual autonomy and desires of both partners, marital rape will persist as a form of violence against women.

This debate requires that we probe deeper. We must be prepared to speak candidly about sex and its place in human life. The law currently states: 'Sexual intercourse or sexual acts by a man with his own wife, the wife not being under fifteen years of age, is not rape.'[11] When sexual intercourse is understood as a form of communion between two people, it is indeed not rape. But how can there be communion without consent? That question is conspicuously absent from our legal imagination.

Marital rape is not criminalized because the law operates on the presumption that it does not, or cannot, exist. Until recently, the courts were equally reluctant to accept that a father could rape his own child. Sexual abuse of children was thought to be committed only by strangers. That mindset has gradually shifted, and the law now recognizes such abuse.

RM: If I understand you correctly, what you're saying is that the most critical analytical contribution feminism has made is to assert that gender relations are predicated on violence—that patriarchy is a relationship of power sustained through violence.

IJ: I'm saying that a central concern of feminist jurisprudence must be to challenge the balance of power that is maintained through violence. The question we must ask, then, becomes how we begin to dismantle violence as a governing principle of social order. That is why I argue that we are still far from engaging in meaningful conversations about equality, fraternity, liberty or even human rights when it comes to women and the law. What we are really speaking about is the need for a structural, systemic shift.

Why did we fight for the Protection of Women from Domestic Violence Act? To confront violence directly and draw a legal line between violence and non-violence. Yet our legal system continues to lack a clear definition of violence itself. We still debate how to define lynching. We have no consistent definition of terrorism. And unsurprisingly, we don't have a clear definition of rape.

Some countries have moved away from the term 'rape' altogether, choosing instead 'sexual abuse', which is often more accurate and encompassing. The act of naming brings us closer to definition, and definition brings us closer to understanding harm.

There is also the violence that resides in the imagination. It lives in the mind and plays out in sexual relations shaped by entitlement rather than mutuality. This is why the argument for decriminalizing marital rape cannot rest on formal equality alone. Marriage itself must be reimagined as an emotional, caring partnership of equals before marital rape can be recognized as a violation of the right to life and liberty.

RM: After thirty or forty years of practising law and thinking about it, what insights have you gained?

IJ: That the law is, and can be, an instrument of social and economic transformation. But also, that women remain its outcasts. I came to understand this fully during the Sabarimala case.

You can work on an issue for years, but sometimes clarity arrives in a single moment. For me, Sabarimala revealed that sex-based discrimination is fundamentally tied to women's outcast status. Their exclusion is social, cultural and legal. It stems from the way fundamental rights fail to extend meaningfully into the domain of personal laws. In that space, the Constitution's guarantee of equality often loses its force.

In India, discrimination cannot be separated from religion. Religion is the hook on which everything hangs. It defines how we pray, how we love and have sex, whom we marry, how we raise our children, how we dress, how we deal with property and even how and what we eat. Religion becomes the framework through which hierarchy is maintained. And the law often reinforces it, instead of disrupting it.

The Supreme Court still has unfinished business when it comes to women. No one can credibly claim that the law has dismantled patriarchy, or any hierarchical structure, so long as religion shapes such intimate aspects of life.

If I were to name one core insight from my years in law, it would be this: We will not build a society free from sex-based discrimination unless the law is disentangled from religion. That applies to all religions. Much of my legal work has focused on stripping personal laws of religious residue. The fight has been long, and the resistance has been constant.

RM: Could secular lawyering be part of the answer?

IJ: Yes, but not on its own. The real imperative is a secular feminist lawyering. In other words, we're not looking for feminist reactionaries. The politics must be both feminist and secular. One of the most challenging cases I've ever argued, precisely because it was so intricately tied to religion, was the 2016 *Shayara Bano vs Union of India* case,[12] commonly known as the triple talaq case. The matter concerned the constitutional validity of the practice of instant triple talaq, by which a Muslim man could unilaterally and irrevocably divorce his wife by pronouncing 'talaq' three times in one sitting. There were two distinct lines of argument: one held that Islam could be interpreted in a way that affirms women's equality and, therefore, instant triple talaq was outside the framework of Islam. I do not subscribe to that view.

The other line of argument was mine: that the law was facially discriminatory and unconstitutional and must be delegitimized and derecognized by the courts and the State. Uncodified laws present a significant challenge to feminism because they rest on so-called custom and tradition and, more crucially, on religion. That is their very nature. Unless you are willing to confront them directly, you won't get anywhere.

Why it is so difficult to challenge uncodified laws? Because it raises a deeper controversy in legal theory: some support codification, while others oppose it. The dangers of codification are obvious. It can freeze social norms in time. Words, once written, may be interpreted differently by different people, but they are fixed on the page. Still, the threat posed by uncodified laws is far greater. These laws are invisible. Their interpretation is controlled by a small group of religious authorities—priests, ulama—who act as exclusive custodians and are capable of issuing highly discriminatory interpretations, shielded by religious authority.

That was my challenge in the triple talaq case: How do you challenge a 'law' that isn't written? Yes, there are scattered commentaries, but nothing you can point to as a statute. There is an irreconcilable conflict between the Sharia and the constitutional guarantee of equality. Sharia is understood as the word of the Prophet but is layered with centuries of interpretation by select scholars. And if we accept a society governed by Sharia, or by divine authority alone, then the fight for feminism, or any meaningful feminist jurisprudence, is already lost. You're back to invoking the fundamental right to religion under the Constitution, at the expense of all other rights.

I chose to challenge an uncodified law, to demand a separation between Sharia and the secular right of a husband to divorce his wife. That right must be both procedurally and substantively fair, because it carries real and significant civil consequences for the woman. This approach was difficult as it had no precedent.

At one point, a judge asked me, 'Ms Jaising, what do you want us to do? Where do you think the judiciary has gone wrong?' And I replied, 'You've gone wrong by recognizing this practice as law.' That's when they paused. They realized that I was arguing that *they*, the court, are the State. And I said, yes, I'm arguing exactly that. It's not just the Government of India declaring this as law. *You* are, too.

So I asked them: Is this what you want to recognize as law? No one fully understood what I was asking, except one judge. He saw that my question was this: What will you do with all these customs and these traditions that stand in conflict with the promise of equality?

3

SECULAR LAWYERING

RM: As we've already discussed, the existence of personal laws based on religion has been a continuing concern for women, for lawyers and for the women's movement. Could you reflect on it further, both as a practising lawyer and as someone who has taken up such cases in court?

IJ: The conflict between personal laws and the fundamental rights we hold so dearly has long beguiled our courts. To begin with, there is lingering judicial uncertainty about what exactly constitutes 'personal law'. Some argue that these are laws governing personal matters, such as marriage, divorce, child custody and inheritance, and they travel with the individual wherever they go. Others maintain that these laws are rooted in religion, i.e., the religion into which one is born, and therefore can never be separated from identity.

In India, these two definitions have, strangely, become fused. We are governed in all such matters by the religion of our birth. This means that our most personal, civil affairs are regulated by religious identity. This raises a constitutional question: Are personal laws truly 'laws' in the constitutional sense, subject to challenge when they violate fundamental rights? Or are they shielded from scrutiny because they are rooted in custom, tradition and faith? If the answer is yes, does a personal law, once reduced to statutory form, cease to be 'personal law' and thus become open to constitutional challenge?

These are not new questions. They go back more than seventy years, to the case of *State of Bombay vs Narasu Appa Mali* in 1951. The case arose when Narasu Appa Mali, a Hindu man charged with bigamy under the Bombay Prevention of Hindu Bigamous Marriages Act, 1946, challenged the law as an unconstitutional interference with religious and personal law practices, and as discriminatory since it applied only to Hindus. The legislation, which declared bigamous marriages void and made them punishable, was examined by a division bench comprising two eminent and progressive judges, Chief Justice M.C. Chagla and Justice P.B. Gajendragadkar.

Two principal arguments were raised against it. First, it was contended that the law singled out the Hindu community in Bombay. It was pointed out that polygamy was both prevalent and legally permissible among Muslims living in the State of Bombay, and Muslim men could marry more than one wife without attracting penal consequences, while a Hindu man doing the same would face prosecution under the new law. Second, it was argued that Muslim personal law, which permits polygamy, had itself become void under Article 13(1)[1] of the Constitution. Article 13(1) provides that all laws in force in the territory of India before commencement of the Constitution, insofar as they are inconsistent with the fundamental rights guaranteed in Part III, shall, to the extent of such inconsistency, be void. It was also argued that the institution of polygamy offended Article 15(1),[2] since it allowed a Muslim man to have more than one wife while restricting a Muslim woman to one husband. The very institution of polygamy was said to be inherently discriminatory against women on the ground of sex.

Essentially, the petitioner—a Hindu man convicted of bigamy—was invoking aspects of Muslim personal law to get his conviction overturned, arguing that there can be no discrimination between Hindu men who are compelled by law to be monogamous and Muslim men who are polygamous.

On the first argument, Chief Justice Chagla said it would be 'difficult to accept ... that polygamy was an integral part of Hindu religion'. Hindu law, he noted, provides for the 'continuation of the line of a Hindu male within the framework of monogamy'.[3] Even assuming that polygamy was recognized in Hindu religious practice, the right of the State to legislate on marriage could not be disputed. Marriage, he said, is a social institution in which the State is vitally interested, and opinion across the world now regards monogamy as a 'desirable and praiseworthy practice'. The State of Bombay, by compelling Hindus to adopt monogamy, was therefore pursuing a measure of social reform. Under Article 25 (2)(b) of the Constitution,[4] the State has the power to legislate for social reform even when it incidentally interferes with the right to freely profess, practice or propagate religion. If the matter had ended there, perhaps the courts would not have been haunted by this case for decades to come.

Both judges rejected the second argument, albeit for different reasons. They agreed that uncodified personal laws did not fall within the definition of 'law' under Article 13(1)(b) and, therefore, could not be challenged for violating the rights under Part III. On the related question of 'custom' and 'usage',[5] Chief Justice Chagla held that both fell within the scope of Article 13 and could be tested against fundamental rights. Justice Gajendragadkar took a narrower view: in his opinion, 'customs' and 'usages' were not laws in the constitutional sense. Only statutory enactments, passed by legislature or any other competent authority, could be brought within the definition of law and be subjected to scrutiny under Article 13. This reasoning meant that the uncodified religious laws, which continued to govern civil rights, would remain outside the reach of constitutional review. The case became a precedent that would shape constitutional debate for decades.

In Chief Justice Chagla's opinion:

- Any custom or usage in force in India that is inconsistent with fundamental rights is void.
- It would be erroneous to state that merely because 'custom' and 'usage' are included within the definition of 'law' under Article 13(1)(b), personal laws must also be included. Custom or usage is a deviation from personal law, not personal law itself. The law recognizes certain institutions that depart from religious texts, or even oppose them because they have been sanctified by custom or usage, but the difference between personal law and custom or usage is clear and unambiguous.
- If Hindu personal law were void under Article 13 by reason of any provision contravening a fundamental right, then there would be no need to provide separately in Article 17[6] and Article 25(2)(b)[7] for those aspects of Hindu personal law that conflict with Articles 14[8] and 15[9]. This indicates

that the Constitution intended to deal with personal law only in certain specified respects.

- The very inclusion of Article 44[10] recognizes the existence of separate personal laws, while Entry 5 in List III of the Concurrent List[11] gives legislatures the power to pass laws affecting them. The scheme of the Constitution, therefore, was to leave personal laws unaffected except where expressly provided, allowing legislatures to reform, codify and ultimately unify them.
- Polygamy is justified, if at all, on social, economic and religious grounds, rarely on grounds of sex. Where it is recognized in a personal law, it is based on considerations vital and compelling to those who believed, and still believe, in the sanctity of their personal law. It would be difficult to say that the institution of polygamy constitutes discrimination against one sex *only* on the basis of their sex.

Justice Gajendragadkar's opinion was as follows:

- Personal laws are in force in a general sense and are administered by courts in India in matters that fall within their purview.
- The expression 'laws in force' in Article 13(1)(b) cannot be read in its broad or general sense. It refers specifically to what may be compendiously described as 'statutory laws'. Unless this condition is met, it would not be legitimate to include personal laws within the meaning of the expression, merely because they are administered by courts in India.

- Personal laws do not draw their validity from any legislation or act of a competent law-making authority in the territory of India. Their foundations of both the Hindu and Mahomedan laws lie in their respective 'scriptural texts'. In Hindu law, the primary sources are the Srutis (primarily, the Vedas) and the Smritis. Over the centuries, these were followed by later texts and commentaries, which came to be relied on by the Hindu law courts. The same is true of Mahomedan law, whose essential source is the Quran.
- If custom or usage having the force of law were truly included in the expression 'laws in force', there would have been no need to provide for the abolition of untouchability through a separate and explicit provision in Article 17. This article not only forbids the practice of untouchability in any form but also makes the enforcement of any disability arising from it an offence punishable by law. As practised among the Hindus, untouchability arose from custom and usage, and in theory and practice, it discriminated against a large section of Hindus on the basis of birth. If such customs were already covered by Article 13(1), they would have been void for violating Article 15(1). In that case, Article 17 would have been wholly unnecessary. It is, then, difficult to accept the argument that custom or usage having the force of law should be regarded as included part of the expression 'laws in force'.
- The legislative history of personal laws shows that they were consistently treated as valid within their own spheres, and courts were directed to apply them in matters falling under their purview. The Constitution itself recognizes their

> existence through Item 5 of the Concurrent List (List III), which includes marriage and divorce; infants and minors; adoption; wills, intestacy and succession; joint family and partition—all domains in which communities, before the Constitution came into force, were governed by their respective personal laws.

It is therefore open to both the State and the Union legislatures to enact laws on these subjects. Yet the term 'personal law' is absent from Article 13. This omission reflects the intention of the Constitution's framers—that personal laws remain outside the ambit of Part III. They were evidently aware that these laws needed reform in several material respects and that over time they ought to give way to a common civil code. But because they did not wish these provisions to be challenged on the grounds of violating fundamental rights, they deliberately excluded personal laws from the expression 'laws in force'.

As you can see, personal laws have enjoyed a kind of immunity from judicial scrutiny. They existed as territories within the Constitution that no one could enter except the clerics. The *Narasu* decision brought into sharp focus the tension between personal laws and fundamental rights, a conflict the courts have been trying to reconcile ever since. The judiciary ceded its powers of review and interpretation of these laws, which govern our civil rights, to the ulama and Hindu priests. This is why I believe that personal laws need to be sanitized of religion if we are to secure a meaningful life of freedom and equality.

As for my own view, the abhorrent practice of triple talaq was, at its core, far more a feminist issue than a religious one. And a feminist issue, after all, is fundamentally a constitutional issue.

The question first arose in my work when we were representing Hasina Khan-led Bebaak Collective[12] in the Shayara Bano case. Shayara Bano was a Muslim woman from Uttarakhand who had approached the Supreme Court in 2016 after her husband divorced her through instant triple talaq. In her petition, she challenged not only talaq-e-biddat but also polygamy and nikah halala, arguing that these practices violated her fundamental rights to equality, dignity and non-discrimination under the Constitution. Her petition became the lead case in what would later be known as the triple talaq case.[13]

Hasina Khan and other Muslim women's organizations, including the Bebaak Collective, intervened to challenge instant triple talaq as unconstitutional and to ensure that the voices of Muslim women themselves were represented in the proceedings. For a while, the case sat dormant. Then, quite suddenly, it was listed during the court's vacation in May 2017. This became the first major case to be heard during the court's summer recess. By then, we had also begun to notice that Shayara Bano herself was growing increasingly warm towards the Bharatiya Janata Party. This, too, reflects one of the defining features of present-day public interest litigation: it is often brought by individuals close to the ruling party in the name of reform, hoping to further their agenda through the courts.

The case was heard by a multifaith bench: Chief Justice Jagdish Singh Khehar, a Sikh; Justice Kurian Joseph, a Christian; Justice Rohinton F. Nariman, a Parsi; Justice U.U. Lalit, a Hindu; and Justice S. Abdul Nazeer, a Muslim.

We saw little active participation from Shayara Bano in the proceedings; in effect, she was represented de facto, though not de jure, by the State. After the judgment, she formally joined the BJP. The then Attorney General of India, Mukul Rohatgi, appeared for the government and argued that triple talaq was unconstitutional.

Unfortunately, religion became the centrepiece of the debate—both for and against this repulsive and arbitrary practice. Counsels laboured over whether triple talaq was integral to Islam, and whether the Quran permits it. The core issue of how the practice demeaned and diminished women never quite took centre stage.

Large sections of the women's movement found themselves in a dilemma and chose to stay away from the debate. The question before them was whether to challenge triple talaq as unconstitutional and risk appearing to support the BJP government's agenda. Yet the injustice of the practice was plain to everyone.

RM: Was this a dilemma for you, too?

IJ: Not for me. It was an opportunity to argue that all personal laws must be consistent with the fundamental rights to equality and dignity. Challenging it at a time when the Muslim minority was already under attack seemed strategically unwise. As a result, the core issue of equality and dignity was left unaddressed.

Meanwhile, the Bharatiya Muslim Mahila Andolan, led by founder and activist Zakia Soman, had already decided to take the issue to the Supreme Court. Drawing on testimonies from women who had borne the brunt of unilateral abandonment by their husbands, the organization approached progressive Muslim lawyers Shadan Farasat and Warisha Farasat to represent them and subsequently sought Anand's assistance to appear on its behalf.

Their strategy was to persuade the court that Islam itself did not sanction triple talaq, and that the practice should be declared bad in law. Indeed, Islam regards triple talaq as sinful. The position that Islam does not recognize triple talaq was supported by respected scholars such as Salman Khurshid, Arif Mohammed Khan and others. The All India Muslim Personal Law Board, which opposed judicial intervention, took a very different view. Even if the practice was considered sinful, it argued, the remedy lay in divine retribution, not judicial correction. The reform in personal law, the board insisted, must come from within the community. Later, Justices Khehar and Nazeer would partially endorse this view in the final judgment.

This is not new. Throughout history, muftis and mullahs have claimed the power to interpret religious law outside the framework of the Constitution. Similarly, the Brahmins have long asserted the authority to define dharma and to anoint kings with the supposed divine right to rule. The struggle over who holds the right to interpret religious texts, and how far those interpretations can be enforced, had already surfaced in the aftermath of the Shah Bano judgment.

In that case, the question was whether Muslim law required a husband to provide maintenance to his divorced wife. The husband's counsel argued that under Muslim personal law, his liability extended only to the period of iddat—three menstrual cycles, or three lunar months, after divorce. The dispute turned on how the relevant verses of the Quran, the ayats, were to be translated and interpreted. The board maintained that the correct reading of the relevant ayat, Ayat 241, referred to 'provision' not 'maintenance', and that even this obligation did not rest upon Muslim men.

The Supreme Court rejected this argument. It held that the ayats left no room for doubt: a Muslim husband is obliged to make provision for, and maintain, his divorced wife. The court also found no conflict between the provisions of Section 125 of the Criminal Procedure Code (CrPC) and Muslim personal law. It dismissed the claim that, under the latter, a husband's responsibility ended with the iddat period, ruling instead that a divorced Muslim woman could seek maintenance under Section 125.

The Bebaak Collective, on the other hand, wanted to engage with the triple talaq case, but without aligning with the State or relying on religious interpretation. My own mandate was different. The role I had set for myself, many years earlier, was to separate religion from personal laws to clear the way towards equality for women. In that effort, the role of the State became critical. Without recognition by the State, triple talaq would not constitute 'law' at all. For me, the issue was never about Muslim law or Islam, but about the very meaning of law and, by extension, of all personal laws. During the hearing, the court confronted a question it had never formally faced before: could Muslim women challenge the constitutionality of laws related to family matters? To say yes would be to accept that all personal laws, including those governing Hindus, must be tested against the guarantees of equality and equal protection under the Constitution.

Each judge on the multifaith bench seemed to wrestle with what such an answer would mean for their own religious identity. This became most evident from the opinions of Chief Justice Khehar and Justice Nazeer. Both held that 'judicial interference with personal law can be rendered only in such manner as provided under Article 25 of the Constitution'—that is, so long as personal laws did not infringe upon 'public order, morality, health and/or the provisions of Part III of the Constitution'.[14] They further held that personal laws could not be challenged on the anvil of Articles 14, 15 and 21 since violations of those provisions could be invoked only against the State. This, despite the fact that Article 25 itself makes the freedom of religion expressly subject to the rest of Part III.

Until this point, the court had sidestepped the question of whether personal laws themselves are constitutional. It's worth recalling that the Muslim Personal Law (Shariat) Application Act, 1937, was enacted during the colonial period at the insistence of sections of the Muslim community, which felt that the Muslims had strayed from the Sharia, and were relying instead on local custom or usage that contradicted it. The act, in effect, drew a line between personal laws based on religious scripture and practices derived from custom.

But this distinction is, I believe, largely illusory. The domain of personal laws is all-encompassing. It extends to marriage, divorce, maintenance, adoption, succession as well as the customs and usages that accompany these matters.

This raises another question: is religion inherited at birth, following a person through life and beyond it? In practice, it often seems so. I have argued cases in which the Christian wife of a Hindu man was denied the right to bury or cremate her husband on the ground that his religion required he be cremated by another Hindu.

In the triple talaq case, my challenge was to bring the bull of constitutional law into the arena and argue that there is nothing truly 'personal' about personal laws.[15] The attorney general, however, stripped the case of its historically gendered social and political dimensions. Adhering strictly to the constitutional framework, he argued that the law was discriminatory on its face because women could not divorce their husbands in the same way.

This was a classic failure to grasp the historical context and the disparate impact of a law that was, by its nature, unjust. Equality cannot mean equal injustice for all.

There was also a striking unwillingness to confront the role of religion in perpetuating the very oppression under challenge. Instead, the argument took on a bleeding-heart tone, asking in effect whether it was not tragic that Muslim women lacked the same legal protection as their Hindu sisters.

When it came to my turn, I said the question was more basic, and that it applied across the board. This is not an issue concerning Muslim women alone. The real question was whether the State would give unquestioning recognition to religious laws, regardless of their content.

During the hearing, senior advocate of the Supreme Court, Kapil Sibal, who was representing the AIMPLB, argued that 'the problem is not religion, the problem is patriarchy'. I laughed and asked, 'And where does patriarchy reside, if not in religion?'

The judgment in 1951 in the Narasu Appa Mali case[16] had held that fundamental rights did not apply to personal laws, since they were not 'laws' within the ambit of the Constitution, originating in religious texts. It's important to remember is that this decision belongs to the early days of the Indian constitutional adjudication, when the courts were not yet fully conscious of the impact fundamental rights could have on people's lives. Moreover, the issue at hand was itself complicated. A Hindu husband, prosecuted for bigamy under the Bigamy Act of 1956, argued that if bigamy was permitted for the Muslims, it should also be permitted for the Hindus. Uneasy about rejecting this argument, the court ended up granting immunity to all personal laws from constitutional challenge. From that point on, custom—not the Constitution—became the governing norm for women in this country. And custom, of course, flowed from religion.

What lay outside statutory law could not be challenged, yet it continued to govern women's lives. My task was to undo this entire framework of thought. The ghost of *Narasu Appa* had to be exorcized.

RM: At any point, did the question of secularism, and of a secular law, come up for discussion?

IJ: It did. During the hearing, Justice Nariman—himself an ordained Parsi priest—asked me, 'How do you intend to challenge religious laws?' That became my opening. I reminded the court that the British, in 1939, had enacted the Muslim Personal Law (Shariat) Application Act of 1937, which declared that in matters of marriage, divorce, adoption and inheritance, the Sharia would apply to Muslims. The irony, I pointed out, was that the act had been passed at the demand of Muslims who felt the Sharia was being diluted by the application of local customs inconsistent with it.

I argued that the State had already recognized the Sharia as law. It couldn't now claim it was not law within the meaning of the Constitution. Although the judgment does not record this argument in full, I could see a visible sense of relief on the judges' faces, as though their consciences were eased in finally stepping into the terrain of personal laws.

The five-judge Constitution bench ultimately held, by a 3:2 majority, that the practice of triple talaq was illegal.

Chief Justice Khehar and Justice Nazeer dissented. They held that triple talaq was integral to the Sunni sect of the Hanafi school and there was 'no doubt' the practice formed part of its 'personal law'. According to them, personal laws were protected under Article 25 of the Constitution and could not be interfered with unless they infringed on the three defined purposes contained in this provision: 'public order, morality, health'.

'It is impossible to conclude,' they wrote, 'that the practice impinges on "public order", or for that matter on "health". It has no nexus to "morality", as well.'[17] They further held that triple talaq could not be challenged under Part III of the Constitution, since Articles 14, 15 and 21 applied only to State actions. In doing so, they ignored my argument that once the State enforces triple talaq, it *a fortiori* becomes law within the meaning of Article 13.

Justice Joseph disagreed with Chief Justice Khehar and Justice Nazeer. He found it 'extremely difficult', as he put it, to accept that triple talaq was integral to the Hanafi school or formed a legitimate part of personal law. Mere longevity, he reasoned, could not validate on a practice that had been expressly declared impermissible. He relied heavily on the 2002 *Shamim Ara vs State of U.P.* judgment, in which the Supreme Court had deprecated triple talaq as contrary to the Quran. On his reading, the Quran—the 'first source of law' in Islam—prohibited the practice. Triple talaq therefore violated Shariat itself.

Justice Joseph went on to outline what he regarded as the 'correct law' of talaq as ordained by the Quran—that it must be exercised for a reasonable cause and preceded by attempts at reconciliation through two arbiters, one from each family. Only if these efforts failed could divorce be effected. In his often-quoted conclusion, he observed: 'What is held to be bad in the Holy

Quran cannot be good in Shariat and, in that sense, what is bad in theology is bad in law as well.'[18]

His reasoning for striking down triple talaq rested chiefly on theological grounds rather than on Articles 14, 15 and 21. In fact, he endorsed Chief Justice Khehar's view that, save for the limitations contained in Article 25, the right to freedom of religion was absolute. Justice Joseph did not venture into the question of whether personal laws form an integral part of Article 25, or whether they are intrinsically immune from challenge as being *ultra virus*—beyond the authority—of the Constitution.

Justice Nariman, writing for himself and Justice Lalit, took a different view. He held that all forms of talaq recognized and enforced by MPL were also recognized and enforced by the Muslim Personal Law (Shariat) Application Act, 1937, including triple talaq as it applied to Sunni Muslims in India. He thus rejected the argument of the MPLB that the 1937 act did not recognize or enforce triple talaq. On the contrary, he held that, 'it clearly and obviously does both', since Section 2 makes triple talaq 'the rule of decision in cases where parties are Muslims'.[19] This was the heart of my argument: the rule of decision must satisfy the requirements of Article 14, 15 and 21.

Justice Nariman made a significant interpretive leap. He stated that since the 1937 act was a pre-Constitutional legislative measure, it fell squarely within the purview of Article 13(1) of the Constitution. Having been enacted before the Constitution came into force, it qualified as 'laws in force' under Article 13(3)(b). Any part found inconsistent with Part III would therefore be rendered void to the extent of that inconsistency. He also expressed reservations about the Narasu Appa judgment, to which I have referred earlier.

Ultimately, Justice Nariman struck down the 1937 act insofar as it permitted triple talaq under Section 2 and, consequently, the practice itself, on the ground that it was 'manifestly arbitrary'. He described the doctrine of 'manifest arbitrariness' as 'something done by the legislature capriciously, irrationally and/or without adequate determining principle. Also, when something is done which is excessive and disproportionate'.[20]

RM: What did you feel about this verdict?

IJ: Justice Nariman's reasoning made it possible to mount future constitutional challenges to personal laws. To that extent, the judgment broke new ground.

Soon after the Shayara Bano judgment, the government—led by the BJP and its National Democratic Alliance coalition—announced its intention to criminalize triple talaq. This move was hailed by many as one reason Muslim women voted for the BJP in the 2019 general elections, though that is not something I can comment on. When the BJP-led NDA returned to power that year, it kept its promise by enacting the Muslim Women (Protection of Rights on Marriage) Act, 2019. The act declared triple talaq illegal and classified it as a criminal offence. It prescribed imprisonment of up to three years and a fine for the husband found guilty. A complaint could be filed only by the wife, or by a relative connected to her by blood or marriage.

Curiously, the National Crime Records Bureau has yet to publish data on how many cases have been registered under this law.

RM: But what are your own views on this?

IJ: There is no doubt in my mind that our civil rights cannot be regulated by religious law. To that extent, I welcome the logic of Justice Nariman's judgment. But that is a far cry from criminalizing triple talaq. That was wholly unnecessary. Muslim personal law has surfaced repeatedly before the Supreme Court. In the 1985 *Mohd. Ahmed Khan vs Shah Bano Begum and Ors*, commonly referred to as the Shah Bano case, the court had held that a divorced Muslim wife could seek maintenance under Section 125 of the CrPC if neglected by her husband. In response, the Rajiv Gandhi-led Congress government enacted the Muslim Women (Protection of Rights on Divorce) Act, 1986, which restricted a divorced Muslim woman's right to maintenance to ninety days after divorce—the iddat period. It was intended to undo the effect of the Shah Bano case.

Around that time, I had met a Muslim woman from Calicut who seemed content with her life—happily married, with three grown children. She came from a wealthy and educated family; her father had once served as a high court judge. She and her husband were returning from Dubai to settle in India and were building a house in Calicut.

One afternoon, as she supervised the construction, a letter arrived. It was written on the letterhead of the Taj Malabar resort in Cochin, and contained only three words: 'talaq, talaq, talaq'. The woman could not believe her eyes. But she stayed calm. A devout Muslim, she couldn't accept that Islam would permit such an act. She resisted the talaq but knew that her marriage was over and that reconciliation was impossible.

She considered going to court to have the document invalidated. Eventually, she decided to seek maintenance instead. The 1986 act provided that a Muslim woman was entitled to a 'reasonable and fair provision to be made and paid during the iddat period'.[21] She decided to argue that the provision must be understood as extending for life. The magistrate's court in Calicut accepted her plea.

Her husband appealed, insisting that the maintenance was limited to the iddat period. The high court rejected his argument, holding that 'fairness' required lifelong maintenance.

Meanwhile, Danial Latifi, Shah Bano's counsel, had already challenged the 1986 act, arguing that Islam did not confine maintenance to the iddat period. By the time the case reached the Supreme Court, Latifi himself had died, though several petitions had gathered around his cause. History had its irony. When the case was finally heard, an NDA government was in power, and the law was defended by its Solicitor General, Harish Salve. The same party that had once accused the Congress of appeasing Muslims through this law now supported its validity in court.

The court ultimately held that Muslim women could seek maintenance either under the general law, Section 125 of the CrPC, or under the 1986 act. Crucially, the phrase 'to be made and paid during the iddat period' was not read as a limitation on duration. Instead, it was understood to indicate when payments were to begin. The amount itself was intended to provide support for life, or as long as the circumstances required.

On behalf of the National Commission for Women, it was again argued that the law could not discriminate between Muslim and Hindu women in matters of maintenance. The court, however, chose not to invoke constitutional principles. Instead, it relied on interpretation and read fairness into the text rather than deriving it from the Constitution. The result was a judgment that secured justice for Muslim women, achieved through a subtle reinterpretation of language rather than through a direct change in the law.

RM: You also took up the Sabarimala Temple entry case …

IJ: I returned to these questions during the Sabarimala Temple case in September 2018. The Travancore Devaswom board, which administers the temple, had for decades upheld a custom that barred women between the ages of ten and fifty from entering the shrine. The restriction was described as physiological, since women of that age are generally understood to be in the menstruating age range. The trust defended the exclusion as intrinsic to its 'institutional worship', grounded in the belief that Lord Ayyappa, the presiding deity, was a Naishtika Brahmachari, committed to lifelong celibacy.

The custom had first been challenged in 2006 by a group called the Indian Young Lawyers Association. The petition, filed by the association's male president, attracted little attention and remained unheard for years. It finally came for hearing during 2017–18 before a five-judge Constitution bench comprising Chief Justice Dipak Misra and Justices R.F. Nariman, A.M. Khanwilkar, D.Y. Chandrachud and Indu Malhotra.

Around this time, a young college student named Nikita Azad came across a remark attributed to the head of the Devaswom Board in response to a question about women's entry by saying, reportedly, that:

> A time will come when people will ask if all women should be disallowed from entering the temple throughout the year. These days there are machines that can scan bodies and check for weapons. There will be a day when the machine is invented to scan if it is the 'right time' [not menstruating] for a woman to enter the temple. When that machine is invented, we will talk about letting women inside.[22]

Shocked by this statement, Nikita, along with some of her friends, launched a social media campaign under the hashtag #HappyToBleed. Later, they also visited slums, spoke with women about menstrual health and sought to challenge the taboos surrounding menstruation. Around the same time, Nikita learned details about the Sabarimala case and approached me to intervene on her behalf.

To me, this so-called custom was discriminatory on two counts: first, by sex; and second, by menstruation within sex. Early in the proceedings, K.K. Venugopal, representing the temple trust, argued that the restriction did not violate Article 15 because it wasn't based on sex but on age—women between the ages of ten and fifty were the only ones barred.

I laughed and said, 'Yes, women only in that age group, not men.'

He replied, 'It's not based on sex but on menstruation.'

I could no longer laugh. 'Yes, sir,' I said, 'but menstruation happens only to women.'

He dropped that argument and moved to the next. The Constitution, he said, protected the right to religion. The trust alone could decide what its faith required, and it had decided that menstruating women could not enter the temple.

This was an open invitation to argue that fundamental rights applied to women, and that any practice contrary to the right to equality and non-discrimination has no place in law. The ghost of Narasu Appa rose again. Article 25 begins: 'Subject to public order, morality and health and to the other provisions of this Part, all persons are equally entitled to freedom of conscience and the right freely to profess, practice and propagate religion.'[23]

Are women not among 'all persons'? I asked. Is it not their right, too, to worship in a temple?

After long hearings, the Supreme Court delivered its verdict on 28 September 2018. By a majority—with Justice Malhotra, the sole woman judge on the bench, dissenting—it held that women did have a right to enter the temple and the exclusionary practice was unconstitutional. Chief Justice Misra, speaking for himself and Justice Khanwilkar, explained that:

- Devotees of Lord Ayyappa are exclusively Hindus and do not constitute a separate religious denomination.
- The right guaranteed under Article 25(1) has nothing to do with gender or, for that matter, certain physiological factors specifically attributable to women.
- The exclusionary practice being followed at the Sabarimala temple violates the right of Hindu women to freely practise their religion.
- The practice of exclusion of women in the age group of ten to fifty years being followed at the Sabarimala temple cannot be regarded as an essential part of the Hindu religion as claimed by the board.

Justice Nariman concurred, holding that the Ayyappa temple at Sabarimala could not claim the status of a religious denomination entitled to protection under Article 26. He emphasized that the exclusionary practice violated Articles 25(1) and 15(1) of the Constitution, which guarantee freedom of religion and equality before the law.

Justice Chandrachud agreed. Article 25, he observed, confers equal entitlement on all persons to profess, practise and propagate religion. The devotees of Lord Ayyappa, in his view, did not constitute a religious denomination under Article 26. He further held that the exclusion of women from the temple was not an essential religious practice. Crucially, he characterized the social exclusion of women based on menstrual status as a form of untouchability, one that was 'anathema' to constitutional values.[24]

Justice Malhotra dissented. She took the view that the guarantee of equality enshrined under Article 14 could not override the rights protected by Article 25. According to her, the Ayyappans, or worshippers at Sabarimala, had made out a 'plausible' claim to qualify as a religious denomination. The 'limited restriction' on the entry of menstruating women, she held, didn't amount to 'untouchability' and therefore fell outside the purview of Article 17.[25] Justice Malhotra ceded to the trust's authority to determine what was integral to its faith, including the question of whether menstruating women could enter the temple. The position, in effect, returned to an earlier constitutional understanding that religious trusts were islands within the Constitution, immune from scrutiny even where their practices clashed with fundamental rights. Fortunately, hers was not the majority decision.

There was still no explicit acknowledgment that *Narasu Appa* had been wrongly decided. Justice Chandrachud did, however, refer to one of my articles, 'The Ghost of Narasu Appa Mali Is Stalking the Supreme Court of India'[26]. He observed that the rationale adopted by Justice Gajendragadkar in the Narasu case, which excluded 'custom and usage' from the meaning of 'laws in force' under Article 13(1), read with Article 13(3)(b), was unsatisfactory, both 'doctrinally' and in light of subsequent Supreme Court precedent. Noting Justice Nariman's reservations in the Shayara Bano case about the continued applicability of *Narasu Appa*, Justice Chandrachud went on to hold that 'custom, usage and personal laws have a significant impact on the civil status of individuals. Those activities that are inherently connected with the civil status of individuals cannot be granted constitutional immunity merely because they may have some associational features which have a religious nature. To immunize them from constitutional scrutiny is to deny the primacy of the Constitution.'[27]

J. Chandrachud's reasoning goes a considerable way towards recognizing that 'custom' and 'usage' fall within the ambit of Article 13 of the Constitution.

RM: Do you concur with him?

IJ: In my view, personal laws occupy the civil domain rather than the religious one. It is, fundamentally, a question of legal taxonomy. The distinction between 'uncodified personal law' and 'custom' or 'usage' is, to my mind, a distinction without a difference. Both operate within the domain of civil and secular rights.

No court has clearly defined what is meant by 'personal laws'. Yet, their scope is set out in Entry 5 of List III in the Concurrent List. This makes clear that personal laws encompass matters relating to marriage and divorce, children, adoption, succession, joint family and partition—many of which remain uncodified. Their uncodified nature does not strip them of their civil character.

Codification itself is a process rooted in colonial governance. Religious laws, codes, practices and customs all form part of what we describe as personal law. However they are classified, whether as custom, usage or personal law, they concern family relations and civil status. Yet they have come to be treated as lying beyond the reach of the Constitution. It is here that the boundary between the public and the private begins to harden, insulating the private from constitutional scrutiny.

This reluctance to interrogate personal laws has allowed the ghost of *Narasu Appa* to continue haunting our courts. Over the years, the Supreme Court has too often preserved the public–private divide through cautious judicial manoeuvres. History, however, tells a different story. Legislation entered this terrain long ago. Dowry was prohibited by statute; sati was abolished; and inheritance was reformed through the Hindu Succession (Amendment) Act, 2005. Even beyond personal law, criminal law has repeatedly crossed into what was once considered the private sphere. Section 498A of the Indian Penal Code, which addresses cruelty within marriage, is one such example. The recurring claim that women have misused this provision echoes an old anxiety (the familiar 'bull in a china shop' argument) that once the Constitution enters the home, it will disturb a fragile and carefully maintained order.

RM: There seems to be a curious overlap here between civil and criminal law …

IJ: Yes. In 2005, the Protection of Women from Domestic Violence Act unambiguously entered the realm of personal law. Neither custom nor usage was beyond its reach. Once it is accepted that the law can intervene in personal matters, even those clothed in religion, how can the courts refuse to strike down practices that deny equality?

As a teenager, I watched my mother live through her monthly confinement. With each cycle, she was shut away in a corner of the house, forbidden to enter the kitchen or join the family puja and made to sleep on the floor. For three days she was untouchable and ate separately. We daughters were spared. As virgins, and therefore 'pure', we were treated like little goddesses. That was the world I ran from. To see it later sanctified in law was unbearable. I could not stand by, and I had to fight to secure some measure of justice for women. When the court finally declared the practice unconstitutional, it felt like justice at last. But it was not the end of the story.

Soon after the judgment, in January 2019, two women from Kerala—Bindu Ammini and Kanaka Durga—successfully climbed the hill to the Sabarimala temple. This was the first time that women of menstruating age had entered the shrine following the Supreme Court's decision. Before they could be stopped, they reached the summit and entered the sanctum. What followed was an eruption of protest across the state. Sections of the Nair community called for demonstrations and bandhs, accusing the Kerala government of betrayal for failing to prevent the women's entry. The priests at the temple conducted a ritual cleansing to rid the shrine of what they described as the 'pollution' caused by the women's presence.

On Bindu's behalf, I approached the Supreme Court, arguing that the priests had committed contempt of court by openly defying its judgment and that Bindu's life was in danger in the aftermath of the protests.

The judges asked, 'What do you want?'

'Protection for Bindu,' I said.

The court directed the police to provide her with security and closed the matter. In doing so, it avoided engaging with the deeper and more troubling question raised by the ritual cleansing itself: whether practices rooted in notions of pollution and purity could survive constitutional scrutiny.

In the days that followed, several organizations asked the court to review its judgment. We were outnumbered. The principal petitioners in the original case had faded from view, and there were rumours that some had reached an accommodation with the temple authorities. The review petitions advanced a new justification for the exclusion, arguing that the taboo was based on science rather than on ideas of untouchability or ritual impurity. A small group of us continued to oppose the review. Then something unexpected occurred.

The review petitions were heard by a new five-judge bench. By this time, Chief Justice Dipak Misra had retired and been succeeded by Justice Ranjan Gogoi. The remaining judges—R.F. Nariman, A.M. Khanwilkar, D.Y. Chandrachud and Indu Malhotra—had all been part of the original bench in the *Indian Young Lawyers Association vs State of Kerala* case.

Justice Malhotra, as expected, reaffirmed her dissent. Justice Khanwilkar, who had earlier joined the majority, changed his position. His reversal altered the balance of the bench. He now sided with the view that the matter required consideration by a larger bench. Justices Nariman and Chandrachud dissented, but they were in the minority.

During the review hearing, I pointed out, despite the court's judgment, several women had either been obstructed from entering the temple or, after entering it, subjected to sustained physical and online abuse. I urged the court to ensure that its decision was implemented in both letter and spirit. And so, the constitutional questions raised by Sabarimala were argued once again in open court.

The majority, comprising Chief Justice Gogoi and Justices Khanwilkar and Malhotra, were of the opinion that the scope of freedom of religion under Articles 25 and 26 needed an authoritative pronouncement by a larger bench. They reasoned that the contours of judicial review in matters of essential religious practices should be settled by at least seven judges. Any such reference, they observed, would also have implications for other pending cases, including those concerning the entry of Muslim women into dargahs and mosques, the entry of Parsi women married to non-Parsis into fire temples, or agiaries, and the constitutional challenge to female genital mutilation among Dawoodi Bohra Muslims.

In dissent, Justice Nariman, joined by Justice Chandrachud, took the view that the only 'narrow question' before the court was whether there were valid grounds to review the Sabarimala decision itself. Questions about the correctness or reach of that decision could be examined when the Supreme Court heard other cases involving the religious practices of Muslims, Parsis and

Dawoodi Bohras. Each bench, they argued, could then decide whether and how the Sabarimala ruling should apply.

After this, Chief Justice S.A. Bobde, who succeeded Gogoi in 2019, constituted a nine-judge bench to consider the questions framed by his predecessor. Several parties objected. They argued that a court sitting in review had no authority to refer questions of law to a larger bench. Under the Supreme Court's own rules, a judgment delivered by five judges can only be reviewed by a bench of equal strength. The nine-judge bench, led by Chief Justice Bobde, dismissed these objections.

RM: How do you read this prevarication, if I may call it that?

IJ: In my opinion, the expansion of the bench served two purposes. First, it created a pathway to undo the Sabarimala judgment itself. Second, it seemed to be a clear attempt to overrule earlier progressive judgments that had curtailed the powers of Hindu religious denominations to matters strictly religious.

The question of women's access to the Sabarimala temple now lies in cold storage. The case has been sidelined and folded into a cluster of matters dealing with religion, religious practices and religious denominations. In the meantime, the state of Kerala has actively prevented women from entering the temple. Bindu, who once stood at its gates, was forced to flee the state for fear of retaliation. She now practises law in New Delhi.

What, then, did we gain from this long journey through constitutional law? There was a judgment worth reading, certainly, but it was undermined by political forces even before it could take effect.

In August 2022, a video surfaced of a conversation between Justices Indu Malhotra and U.U. Lalit during a visit to the Sree Padmanabhaswamy temple in Thiruvananthapuram. In the video, Justice Malhotra was heard remarking that 'Communist governments … all over have taken over. All over. Only Hindu temples.'[28] Referring to the Padmanabhaswamy temple, she was also heard saying that she, along with Justice Lalit, had halted such takeovers by governments like Kerala's, which she alleged takes over temples, specifically Hindu temples, 'for revenue'. She added that she wouldn't allow this.

The decision of the larger bench on the review petitions remains pending.

RM: Strangely, or perhaps not so strangely, there is another overlap here, between personal law and family law.

IJ: To my mind, a single thread runs through personal law—the enduring grip of religion over the domain of family law. One clear illustration is the 1999 case involving the writer Githa Hariharan.

Githa wished to deposit a sum of money with the Reserve Bank of India in her minor son's name. The bank refused, saying that it could accept such a deposit only from the child's natural guardian, that is, his father. Shocked, Githa came to me for legal advice. At first glance, the matter seemed straightforward. The Hindu Minority and Guardianship Act, 1956, stated plainly that the father is the natural guardian of a minor child and, only after him, the mother. The same law designated the mother as the natural guardian of an illegitimate child. On its face, this was discriminatory against a mother within marriage.

We decided to challenge the law in the Supreme Court. Harish Salve appeared for the RBI, which maintained it could not accept a deposit from the mother. Around the same time, the Indian scholar Dr Vandana Shiva, who faced the prospect of losing custody of her son to her husband, also approached the court to challenge the same provision. She argued that while the mother bore the responsibility of giving birth to and raising a child, the law vested guardianship in the father. Rights, she said, could not be divorced from responsibilities; they must rest together. Once again, the court chose a middle path rather than the clear route to equality. It ruled that the law did not bar the mother from acting as the natural guardian. The phrase 'in the case of a boy or an unmarried girl—the father, and after him, the mother' under Section 6(a) of 1956 act, it ruled, did not mean only after the father's death.[29] It could also apply to situations where the father had neglected the child. In such circumstances, the mother could be recognized as the natural guardian.

The court explained its reasoning as follows:

> The word 'after' need not necessarily mean 'after the lifetime'. In the context in which it appears in Section 6(a), it means 'in the absence of', the word 'absence' therein referring to the father's absence from the care of the minor's property or person for any reason whatever. If the father is wholly indifferent to the matters of the minor even if he is living with the mother or if by virtue of mutual understanding between the father and the mother, the latter is put exclusively in charge of the minor, or if the father is physically unable to take care of the minor either because of his staying away from the place where

> the mother and minor are living or because of his physical or mental incapacity, in all such like situations, the father can be considered to be absent and the mother being a recognized natural guardian, can act validly on behalf of the minor as a guardian. Such an interpretation will be the natural outcome of a harmonious construction of Section 4 and Section 6(a) of the HMG Act [Hindu Minority and Guardianship Act, 1956], without causing any damage to the language of Section 6(a).[30]

In Githa's case, the Supreme Court once again showed its reluctance to strike down a personal law that was *ex facie* discriminatory and violative of the principle of equality. There was no real basis for treating this as something other than 'law', yet its characterization as a personal law allowed the court to remain hands-off. It held that the RBI was wrong to insist on an application signed by the father or supported by a court order, particularly where there was a joint letter from the parents indicating mutual consent. The court directed the RBI to accept the mother's application and advised the bank to frame suitable procedures in line with its judgment.

The case has had a long afterlife. It brought tangible change for separated and divorced women. Schools started admitting children without insisting on the father's signature. Passports were issued to children of divorced mothers at the mother's request, without requiring an application from the father. Yet the larger goal of constitutional equality for all women is still unmet. Despite repeated recommendations by law commissions, successive governments have failed to amend the statute. Hindu law continues to designate the father as the child's natural guardian. The grip of religion over women's intimate lives remains firmly in place.

RM: One of your most talked-about cases concerning the rights of women was on behalf of Mary Roy …

IJ: Mary's case involved a different set of laws governing Christian women. Mary Roy, who had fled her husband with her two children, returned to Kerala seeking refuge in her maternal home and chose to live in Ooty, in a house owned by her family. One day, the police showed up at her door with an order directing her to vacate the premises. Her brother had sent them, alleging trespass and demanding possession of the house.

Panicked, Mary went to the only lawyers she knew in the city, King & Partridge. They told her that while they knew little about personal laws of inheritance, no one could be dispossessed of property except by procedure established by law. They advised her not to vacate. That was all she needed to hear.

Later, I told her it was the best possible advice she could have received. It saved her life and the lives of her two children. Once the immediate threat of eviction had passed, Mary began to investigate her rights as a daughter in her ancestral property. That was when she encountered the Travancore Christian Succession Act, 1092. The act denied daughters an equal share in the property of an intestate. She was entitled only to one-fourth of the son's share or ₹5,000, whichever was less. Even this limited entitlement could be denied only if stree dhan—property or wealth given to a woman at the time of marriage—had been given or promised. Mary came from a wealthy, coffee-growing, landed community. Her family owned extensive immovable property, to which she could lay no claim under this law. She decided to challenge the law on the basic principles of equality—her right, and her children's right, to life and liberty.

Over time, Mary went on to establish herself as an educationist and set up a well-known school, Corpus Christi, in Kottayam, Kerala. But she didn't give up the claim to the ancestral property. She filed a petition in the Supreme Court.[31] This time, too, I believed it was an open-and-shut case.

The matter was decided by a bench of Justice P.N. Bhagwati and Justice R.S. Pathak. Instead of striking down the Travancore Christian Succession Act as unconstitutional, the court took a different route. It held that the act, having been enacted by a Part B state,[32] had ceased to exist once those states were abolished. Mary was therefore governed by the Indian Succession Act, 1925, which applied uniformly to Christians and entitled daughters to an equal share with their brothers.

But once again the court skirted the larger question: Are personal laws subject to the Constitution? That question still hangs unresolved. It is hardly surprising, then, that when I hear calls for a 'common civil code', I find myself wondering whether the courts might one day reverse course and declare that personal laws can be altogether abolished.

In this context, one case remains especially poignant.

In 2010, a Parsi woman, Goolrokh M. Gupta, who was married to a Hindu, approached the Gujarat High Court challenging the ban on her entry into the Parsi fire temples and the Tower of Silence[33] after marrying outside the community.[34] Her father was still alive—he was eighty-seven at the time—but she wanted to ensure that she would be allowed to participate in his last rites when the time came. She had appealed to the Parsi panchayat, which ran the religious site, seeking permission. They refused, saying that by marrying a Hindu she had forfeited her right to enter the fire temple, even for her own father's ceremonies. It was then that she went to court, arguing that her marriage should have no bearing on her right to worship or to perform her familial duties.

In a disturbing judgment, the high court held that on marriage a woman acquires the religion of her husband. I had never encountered a ruling like it. Where was this coming from? It seemed to me the judges had been influenced by the Doctrine of Coverture, a principle of common law from medieval England, stating that a woman's legal identity merged with that of her husband's on marriage. It was the same thinking that underpinned Exception 2 to Section 375 of the IPC, which assumes that a wife cannot charge her husband with rape because, through marriage, she has irrevocably given herself to him. That logic was now being extended to all areas of personal law—to the point where it was used to deny a woman the right to participate in her own father's funeral rites.

Where does this leave us? Hindu, Muslim, Christian and Parsi women have all gone to court seeking equality before the law and equal protection under it, challenging laws that are plainly discriminatory. Have they received it? Each time, the courts found a way to avoid the issue. The immunity of personal laws from constitutional scrutiny remains intact. The ghost of *Narasu Appa* has yet to be laid to rest.

RM: I want to ask you about the recent Uniform Civil Code regulation introduced by the state of Uttarakhand, which makes it mandatory for live-in couples to register their relationship, with punitive consequences if they don't. Is this not violative of the right to privacy? What, in your opinion, can serve as a legal restraint on a regulation like this?

IJ: Early on in our conversation, I suggested that several of these questions can't really be answered unless we have what one might call, for want of a better term, a theory of justice and a theory of governance. Justice is, of course, a demand placed on the State. But it is also inseparable from what we value. Our values shape our understanding of justice, because we seek justice for what we hold dear, and some values are non-negotiable. If I believe in liberty, equality and fraternity, those beliefs are not open to question. The Constitution is meant to be the instrument through which those values are realized. If I say the Constitution is my home, then it must be a home I build that I actually want to live in. From that standpoint, liberty includes the right to live as I choose. No power on earth should dictate how I live my life, so long as I don't harm another person.

If I choose to live with someone, if I recognize that person as my family—which is, after all, the basis of any community—I'm choosing the community to which I belong, even if that community consists of only two people. The sex of one's partner is irrelevant; this is your community.

That brings us to the nature of rights. At its core, the Constitution is meant to restrain the arbitrary exercise of State power. That is why we have fundamental rights. Viewed in this light, the State has no authority to intrude on whom you choose to live with, how you choose to live or when you choose to live together. Privacy is often invoked in this context, but it is really shorthand for the domain of autonomy. At stake here are both the individual's privacy and their capacity to make autonomous choices and exercise agency.

For these reasons, I see such rules and regulations as wholly unconstitutional. They violate a range of fundamental rights that exist precisely to limit State power. Instead, we're witnessing the reverse, with the State entering our homes and becoming increasingly intrusive.

There is, of course, one important qualification. The State has an interest in protecting vulnerabilities. In a live-in relationship, for example, where children are involved, neither partner can simply walk away. Responsibility for their care must be assumed, and that responsibility rests with the parents. In that limited sphere, the State may intervene to say the individuals who chose the relationship must protect those who are vulnerable. It can require that an individual cares for XYZ or that they refrain from violence. To that extent, the boundary between public and private can be crossed. Beyond that narrow purpose, a law of this kind is indefensible.

RM: Do you think it will be challenged?

IJ: It has already been challenged in the Delhi High Court on behalf of an individual litigant. The challenge rests primarily on two grounds. First, that the regulation excludes tribal communities from the protection of equal rights. Second, that it infringes the right to privacy. There is no possibility of this law going unchallenged. The right it interferes with is intensely personal. Privacy, in fact, may not fully capture what is at stake, as the subject of regulation lies even closer to the skin. It encompasses intimacy in its most fundamental form. The State is regulating the right to have a relationship, to have sex with a person of your choice. Then it's not just a regulatory measure.

It's a political statement. It's a declaration of where the moral and political priorities of the State stands today, intended quite plainly as a deterrent to live-in relationships on moral grounds.

RM: On a related note, I'd like to ask you about something you've often said—that when we talk about switching faiths, the term should be 'adoption' rather than 'conversion'. Could you expand on that idea? What, in your view, would be the legal, political and social implications of such a shift?

IJ: Anti-conversion laws have a pre-colonial history. Several princely states had laws that prevented Hindus from converting to Christianity. These were laws dealing with apostasy. Two examples are the Raigarh State Conversion Act of 1936 and the Surguja State Apostasy Act of 1942, followed by a further enactment in 1945. Post-Independence laws pursue the same objective, though they are framed as 'freedom of religion' laws. Their purpose and effect are similar. They target the priest who performs the ceremony and are designed to have a chilling effect on religious choice. Faith, however, is a matter of conscience. Rituals—what these laws describe as 'conversion'—are performed by a priest and serve only as evidence of a change of faith. This is why I insist that the act of adopting a religion must be separated from the ceremony commonly described as conversion.

The language of 'conversion' rests on an assumption that a person is born into the religion of their parents. This is nothing more than a legal fiction, because there is no element of choice involved. By contrast, when a person chooses to adopt a faith, that choice is an act of conscience and of agency. That is why I describe it as adoption of a faith. The ceremony of conversion ordinarily performed by a priest of the religion the individual has chosen merely gives expression to that choice. It is, therefore, necessary to distinguish between the two: the act of adoption, which belongs solely to the individual, and the ritual ceremony, which is evidence of that adoption. To describe the individual as 'converting' is, in this sense, a misuse of language.

The underlying assumption of all such laws is that we are all born Hindus, and that adopting another faith therefore amounts to conversion. This assumption also explains expressions such as 'love jihad' and 'ghar wapasi'. The former is a politically charged term used to allege that Muslim men systematically lure Hindu women into marriage in order to convert them, a claim that has repeatedly surfaced in public discourse despite the absence of credible empirical evidence. The latter, meaning 'homecoming', is used to describe efforts to convert individuals, often from Muslim or Christian communities, back to Hinduism, on the theory that they were originally Hindus who had strayed. These are political categories, not legal, as there is no presumption in law that we are all born Hindu. The term apostasy more accurately captures what these laws are concerned with, as did the pre-colonial laws that sought to prevent Hindus from renouncing their faith in favour of Christianity. Those princely-state laws were directed, in particular, at stopping tribal communities from adopting Christianity. Independent India modelled its anti-conversion laws on this framework.

The issue first reached the Supreme Court when such laws in Madhya Pradesh[35] and Orissa[36] were challenged by Christian missionaries in the 1970s. In *Reverend Stanislaus vs State of Madhya Pradesh*, the petitioners questioned the validity of state laws regulating religious conversions. The 1977 judgment held that there is no fundamental right to convert another person to one's own religion. Its reasoning was that the freedom of religion under Article 25 applies equally to all faiths and must be exercised in a manner consistent with the freedom of others. As the court put it, 'What is freedom for one is freedom for the other in equal measure, and there can therefore be no such thing as a fundamental right to convert any person to one's own religion.'[37]

In my view, this argument was directed at a paper tiger. No one had claimed a fundamental right to convert another person. An individual's fundamental right to choose and adopt a religion, a right that unquestionably exists, had been asserted. If the chosen religion requires certain rituals to complete the act of adoption, those rituals form part of the right to freely choose one's faith. It is well known that religions such as Christianity and Islam prescribe specific rituals to welcome new members into the community. These rituals affirm the individual's choice and allow full participation in the religious life of the group. If such rituals are criminalized, the right to adopt another religion is effectively denied.

In practice, this amounts to a complete prohibition on choosing any faith other than the one inherited at birth. The question of 'interference' with anyone's freedom of religion does not arise. The ritual act of conversion is not an intrusion into another's conscience. It is an affirmation of the individual's choice to belong to a particular faith.

In everyday language, we often use the word 'convert' to describe the act of adopting a new religion. That casual usage has carried over into legal reasoning, and it has led to a persistent confusion of thought in judicial decisions.

It is one thing to insist that the adoption of a faith should not involve coercion or fraud. It is quite another to suggest, as the court does, that there is no right for a religious official to perform the act of conversion itself. More recent laws enacted by various states over the past decade go even further. They treat the provision of education or the prospect of marriage as forms of allurement or fraud, and criminalize them when they accompany a change of faith.

When a change of faith upon marriage is characterized as an 'allurement', the true object of these laws becomes clear: to prevent interfaith marriages. Indian law recognizes marriages between two people of the same faith as valid. It also recognizes marriages between people of different faiths when solemnized under the Special Marriage Act, 1954. It is for the couple to decide under which legal framework they wish to marry. Where a marriage is performed under personal law, one partner may choose to adopt the faith of the other. To describe this choice—often made out of conscience or love—as 'allurement' is to interfere directly with the couple's fundamental right to decide how they wish to live their lives.

These laws are commonly justified on the ground that conversions may lead to a breach of public order. In my view, that reasoning is deeply flawed. An individual's decision to change faith does not pose a threat to public order by itself. The court has repeatedly held that the State's duty is to prevent breaches of public order. Experience also shows that such breaches are seldom the result of individual acts of conscience. On the contrary, vigilante violence by right-wing Hindu groups has often accompanied the performance of interfaith marriages, with spurious justifications such as the need to prevent 'love jihad' offered to legitimize that violence. This suggests that the real object of these laws is less about maintaining public order and more about preventing apostacy by Hindus to other faiths.

A person's decision to adopt a new faith is a matter of conscience and lies beyond the legitimate reach of the State. It is, in fact, protected by Article 25 itself. Conversion, by contrast, refers to the public ceremonies that may accompany the adoption of a faith. The language of 'to convert' is therefore misleading in discussions of freedom of conscience or freedom of religion. It collapses a personal act of belief into a ceremonial act of recognition.

Religion cannot be assigned by operation of law. It can only be acquired, or relinquished, through an active decision of the individual. Your question arises, of course, in the context of what are commonly referred to as 'love jihad' laws. The term itself has been mobilized into the public discourse by the BJP as part of a broader anti-Muslim rhetoric. Fear-mongering, however, cannot supply constitutional legitimacy. Conversion and adoption carry different meanings. This distinction remains important.

With the coming into force of the Constitution, one might have expected the debate over anti-conversion laws to evolve, or even recede. The Constitution guarantees freedom of religion to all under Article 25. It is a secular document. It recognizes no state religion, and blasphemy finds no place in our penal law.

The fact that religion involves ritual and collective practice does not change the nature of the right itself. Freedom of religion remains an individual right. It is individuals who are the bearers of this freedom. The rights to profess, practise and propagate religion flow from that premise. Temples, churches, mosques and agiaries exist to facilitate the collective exercise and expression of an *individual right*. They cannot define or limit it.

The phrase 'love jihad' has no legal meaning and should have no place in civil discourse. Yet, recent 'freedom of religion' laws directly target interfaith marriages. When two individuals of different faiths choose to marry, one may voluntarily adopt the religion of the other. To label this act as love jihad is a gross distortion of fact as well as a denial of both individuals' agency. To criminalize such a choice is to manufacture a crime where none exists.

A person is born into the religion of their parents and is presumed to belong to that faith. There is little choice involved in the matter. That presumption can, however, be displaced by how the child is brought up; parents may opt not to raise their child in any particular religion. In interfaith families, the child is usually presumed to belong to the father's faith. On attaining adulthood, though, every individual has the right to choose their own religion—or to reject religion entirely. The freedom to be agnostic or atheist is also protected under Article 25, which guarantees the freedom of religion and of conscience.

It's worth noting that the Constitution never uses the word 'convert'. The expression 'to adopt another religion' better captures the essence of what freedom of conscience entails, and aligns more closely with the right to freely profess, practise and propagate one's faith.

After all, the right to freedom of religion would be hollow if it didn't include the freedom to adopt a religion of one's choice or to renounce religion altogether. This understanding must guide our approach to the so-called anti-conversion laws.

To my mind, there is no real conundrum here; it is one that our courts have created. Too often, they have been confined by the narrow text of Article 13, overlooking the broader constitutional vision. The Constitution places the individual at the forefront: it guarantees civil and political rights in Part III and aspires to achieve social and economic justice through Part IV. Religion, therefore, is not the focal point of the Constitution. The Constitution must remain supreme. Religious texts derive legitimacy from the Constitution, not through any community's authority. Where religious doctrine conflicts with the principles enshrined in Part III, the Constitution must prevail.

Hindutva seeks to propagate the notion that there are two sources of authority—and that religious texts hold primacy over the Constitution. This is a fundamental falsehood. As stated, the right to religion is guaranteed *under* the constitution, not *outside* it. The attempt to elevate any sacred text above the Constitution is a political project. And yet, this project can creep into judicial reasoning when judges use religious texts to interpret the law. This tendency must be firmly resisted if the secular character of the Constitution is to be preserved.

RM: Would you advocate something like a gender-just family code that could reconcile some of these anomalies?

IJ: To begin with, we need a theory of justice to answer this question. For me, that understanding has been shaped by Buddhist thought. Buddhism is not founded on the idea of a god or a sacred text. Indeed, if this country ever had an ancient philosophy of equality, it was in Buddhism. Neither God nor religion should have any role in a gender-just family code. Such a code deals with civil matters and must be premised on the guaranteed right to equality in all matters public and private. We also need a coherent theory of governance. The State's interference in matters of family, marriage, adoption and child custody should be limited to ensuring legitimate state interests. These may include preventing the abandonment of vulnerable partners in a marriage, ensuring equitable distribution of matrimonial property and securing the appropriate care and maintenance of children. All other aspects relating to choice—love, emotional ties, questions of morality or sexual choices—must be left to individual conscience.

As citizens, we must have the freedom to form families of our own choosing and define them as we see fit. These family formations—however diverse—deserve equal recognition from the State, just as conventional families do. In other words, religion, custom, culture and so-called tradition should have no place in framing a gender-just code. Of course, human beings carry memory and tradition as part of their psyche. The form a recognized union takes, whether solemnized through Islamic, Hindu or Christian rites, can remain a matter of personal preference. But the substance of that relationship must be entirely independent of religion, culture or tradition.

As I have said before, from the moment of our independence, there has been only one legal culture—that of the Constitution. In this culture, religion plays no role. This understanding aligns perfectly with the constitutional limits placed on religion itself: public order, health and morality.

It is true that gender-discriminatory personal laws persist across religious communities. Instead of introducing a single, uniform gender-just code, we could consider an incremental approach:

amending the existing personal laws that apply to different communities to ensure women are treated equally and uniformly in matters such as marriage, divorce, maintenance, custody and guardianship, adoption, succession and inheritance. This is, in fact, the course of action endorsed by the Law Commission of India in its 'Consultation Paper on Reform of Family Law'.[38] The decision in *Narasu Appa* does not stand in the way of such reform; on the contrary, it exhorted the legislature to intervene so that personal laws do not violate Part III of the Constitution. A key feature of this case is its recognition that once personal laws are codified into statutory form, they become subject to constitutional scrutiny.

4

BODILY INTEGRITY

RM: I'd like to ask you now about the sexual harassment cases you have argued, and what they meant to you in your quest for justice for the women concerned.

IJ: Let me focus on two cases that were especially significant for me: those of Rupan Deol Bajaj, an Indian Administrative Service officer, and Ms X, a judge of the district court in Madhya Pradesh.

I first met Rupan while working in the chambers of a constitutional lawyer in Delhi. During the hearings, the senior advocate asked me to take over her case, and I readily agreed. It was the first case of its kind to reach the Supreme Court. Rupan had invoked Sections 354 and 509 of the IPC, i.e., all provisions dealing with outraging the modesty of a woman. Although these provisions had been used earlier, they largely involved cases of assault against young girls or children. This was before the Protection of Children from Sexual Offences Act, 2012, a law aimed at safeguarding children from sexual abuse and exploitation, and before the Vishaka judgment,[1] which laid the foundation for workplace sexual harassment law in India. There was no law on sexual harassment at the workplace or elsewhere, and only a few state laws addressing 'eve-teasing', or sexual harassment of women in public places.

Rupan was a high-ranking IAS officer. The incident occurred on 18 July 1988 at a dinner party hosted by Surinder Lal Kapur, a senior Punjab bureaucrat, at his home in Sector 16, Chandigarh. Rupan and her husband were among the guests. Also present were several high-ranking officials, including K.P.S. Gill, then director general of police, Punjab. By then Gill had acquired a reputation—lauded in the press and by the middle class—for his role in ending militancy in Punjab through encounter killings, even as he stood trial for multiple cases, including murder. The rule of law, suspended in the process, was of no concern.

As part of her professional responsibilities, Rupan was expected to attend such functions, which were often family affairs. That evening, the women were seated separately, most of them wives of serving officers. When Rupan joined them, she found Gill beside her, drink in hand. As she prepared to sit, she felt his hand run down her bottom. Startled, she drew her chair away. When she tried to sit again, the same touch. Outraged, she spoke up, found her husband and the two of them walked out of the party, registering their protest as they left.

Her legal ordeal began soon after. She demanded an apology from Gill and wrote to the governor, requesting an inquiry into his behaviour. The governor was Siddharth Shankar Ray, a senior lawyer associated with the Congress party and remembered for having advised Mrs Gandhi to declare the Emergency in 1975. He conducted an investigation of sorts, but instead of recommending action, merely issued Gill a warning not to drink in public. That 'warning' later became notorious, surfacing in court as evidence and, eventually, as the only disciplinary action ever taken against him.

To say that Rupan faced a hostile press would be an understatement. Gill was, after all, widely celebrated as a national hero. Editorials dismissed her complaint outright. 'What's a slap on the back?' they asked. Isn't this part of water-cooler workplace culture? Why take offence at something so minor? Her use of the word 'back' rather than 'bottom' in her complaint was relentlessly used against her. During one court proceeding, Gill's lawyer and old friend K.T.S. Tulsi turned to me and asked: 'What's a pat on the back, Ms Jaising? Right now, in court, if I tap you on the back, would you object?'

'Try it,' I replied, 'and see what you get from me.'

The first major obstacle was the refusal to register her complaint. The FIR that was eventually filed was weak and headed for closure. None of the women seated near her that evening came forward—they were wives of serving officers, and Gill was their husbands' superior. Rupan's husband, who stood by her resolutely and faced retaliation through false corruption charges, filed a private complaint. That too went nowhere. The criminal case against Gill was ordered closed. The criminal proceedings were closed. Rupan challenged this in the high court, but the court, seemingly overawed by Gill's reputation, declined to intervene. She then moved the Supreme Court, at which point I entered the case.

In a history-making verdict, the late Justice Ajoy Kumar Mukherjee held that 'outraging the modesty' of a woman could and did include 'outraging the dignity of a woman'.[2] He ruled that Rupan's testimony, if found credible, was sufficient in and of itself, and that the absence of witnesses was not grounds for dismissing her complaint.

Justice Mukherjee reconceptualized modesty to include an assault on a woman's dignity. Until then, the term had been understood only in terms of the sexual, not necessarily as a matter of undermining dignity. It's only after his verdict that the prosecution began and the case moved to the magistrate.

The Supreme Court's ruling sent Gill's case before a magistrate's court in Chandigarh. Rupan stood as her sole witness. She held to her account of that evening. Of great significance to me, and to the court, was what followed the first assault: Rupan got up and moved her chair away from Gill. That act clearly indicated his advances were 'unwelcome'—a necessary element in cases of sexual harassment.

In his defence, Gill summoned the former governor to testify. Faced with the record, Ray acknowledged that on receiving Rupan's complaint, he had summoned Gill and counselled him not to drink in public again. In his assessment, that admonishment was punishment enough.

The trial concluded in Rupan's favour. An unusually bold and upright magistrate did what the high court had hesitated to do. He sentenced Gill to three months' imprisonment for outraging the modesty of a woman, and two months' rigorous imprisonment for speech and gestures intended to insult the modesty of a woman. The sentences were to run concurrently, amounting to a term of three months in jail.

Predictably, Gill appealed to the sessions court. I appeared once again on Rupan's behalf. The evidence was overwhelming. The sessions court upheld the conviction but converted the sentence to six months' probation, along with a directive that Gill not consume alcohol in public during that period. The purpose was obvious. Probation softened the stigma of punishment and kept the door ajar to future appointments. By then Gill had retired. Even so, he was still considered a national asset and astonishingly continued to be consulted on counterterrorism. Much later, I asked the sessions judge why he had reduced the sentence. He replied that with probation, Gill could continue serving the nation, but a conviction with imprisonment would have barred him. In his eyes, a woman's dignity was negotiable.

Gill then appealed to the high court, which upheld both the conviction and the sentence. Rupan, too, appealed. Gill maintained that he was not guilty, arguing that even the probation conditions should be expunged. By this time, the six months had elapsed. What remained was the question of guilt. I appeared once again for Rupan, this time before the Supreme Court.

The case came before Justices K.G. Balakrishnan and B.N. Srikrishna. I remember Rupan asking me: 'The Supreme Court has said in the Vishaka judgment that a woman should be on an internal committee, why then is there no woman judge in my case'? I answered, 'Because, at this point, there is no woman judge in the Supreme Court of India.'

The hearing proceeded. Once again Gill was represented by K.T.S. Tulsi. His defence this time relied on the doctrine of *de minimis*, arguing under Section 90 of the IPC that the harm caused was so minor that no reasonable person would treat it as an offence. I countered that any 'reasonable woman' would complain of being felt up and down her bottom. The judges upheld the conviction.

Rupan was unequivocal: she sought no retribution, only public acknowledgement of what had happened. Whether Gill was considered a 'national hero' was irrelevant to her. She has said, on record, that had he apologized to her publicly, she would never have gone to court. But he refused. For her, a public apology would have been justice. For me, too, this judgment represented justice served. I did not encourage her to appeal the probation term. Like her, I believed that justice lay in the formal recognition of the wrong.

To this day, the late K.P.S. Gill is celebrated in some circles as the man who 'ended terror and separatism in Punjab'.[3] Each time, I feel compelled to remind people that he was no hero. He sexually assaulted a serving woman officer.

Rupan never spoke publicly about K.P.S. Gill again. After retirement, she returned to her passions: bonsai and the Rock Garden in Chandigarh, which she had helped conceptualize. Years later, I asked her why she had fought that battle and why she hadn't simply let it go. She replied that she was in charge of a large workforce, and if she had stayed silent, every employee, from the peon upwards, would have believed she was fair game. For her, the fight was about maintaining command with dignity in a male-dominated workplace.

Her pursuit of justice began in 1988 and concluded only in 2005. The case stands as a stark reminder of how prolonged the Indian justice system can be. For once, delayed justice did not amount to its denial. She was ultimately vindicated even if Gill continues to be remembered as a hero in the public imagination.

RM: In the judge *Ms X's* case, too, a senior male colleague was implicated, I recall. But how did you come to represent her?

IJ: She was referred to me by a friend of hers in United Nations Women. But I already knew about her situation.

On 4 August 2014, *The Times of India* carried a front-page story about a district judge in Madhya Pradesh who had written to the Chief Justice of India and the President of India, alleging sexual harassment by a sitting high court judge of the state.[4] The story sent shockwaves through the legal fraternity, including the judiciary. It was the first time that the institution's dirty secrets had broken into public view. Until then, there had only been murmurs about secretaries or junior staff members hinting at such harassment. No one had come forward with a formal complaint. It took a sitting woman judge to speak out for the institution to even pay attention. The impact was seismic.

I read her complaint with care. It was lucid and precise, grounded in Article 15 of the Constitution. She raised a clear contradiction that on the one hand, the judiciary urges more women to join its ranks in its public commitments and on the other, women in the profession face sexual harassment severe enough to push them out. She herself had resigned, unable to find a forum in which to lodge her complaint. There was no system of redress available to her.

Most of the sexual harassment matters I had dealt with until then had involved women who were still at their posts, fighting from within. In contrast, in the US, such cases are more often brought by women who resign and then seek compensation for the harassment they had endured—often successfully. In India, whenever I suggested that women pursue compensation, I'm met with reluctance. They fear being labelled 'gold-diggers'. The culture of treating damages as a legitimate claim against sexual harassment has never taken hold. Instead, women who face intense bias are accused of 'misusing the law'. As a result, many step back from claiming damages and compensation, even when they have been plainly wronged.

Ms X's case was the first I took on in which the complainant had already resigned. That fact alone posed a challenge. But then again, she wanted a formal acknowledgment that she had been sexually harassed, and that it was this harassment that had forced her out of the judiciary. She was not looking for compensation. Ms X wanted it recognized that she had been denied the chance to serve her country. Like Rupan, she came from a family with ties to the armed forces and saw her work as a form of public service. With her confidence, clarity and sense of purpose—as a lawyer and as a citizen—she might have excelled in legal practice. But she chose to be a judge. Perhaps her disadvantage was that she took her rights seriously, especially her right not to be sexually harassed at work. As a student, she had been the first woman vice-president of the National Students' Union of India. She knew what it meant to assert one's rights. I have little doubt these qualities, which would have been an asset as a judge, were viewed as 'insubordination' and, ultimately, weighed against her.

She was proud of her work. Her annual confidential reports were consistently positive. Later, this would be turned against her, the argument being that she couldn't have been victimized, since the very judge she accused had given her favorable assessments. She was appointed to head the sexual harassment committee for court staff, assigned cases involving violence against women and was noted in the press for the speed and clarity of her judgments. Her decisions were often reported with approval. She was in the public eye, and that visibility seems to have drawn the unwanted attention of her supervising judge.

She told me she had first noticed his unusual interest at public functions and had grown cautious. 'A woman always knows when a man has a buri nazar [a predatory gaze],' she told me. The harassment followed soon after.

Unlike other judges, she was denied the service of a peon at her residence. When she raised the matter with the district judge, she was told to 'complain to the administrative judge'—the very man she accused. At crucial moments, just as she was due to write important judgments, her stenographer would be withdrawn. It was a deliberate attempt to obstruct her work. A supervisory judge was sent to observe her in court, evidently to unsettle her. On those days, she told me, she would not even get up to use the toilet; she worked through the break, fearing that the visiting judge might record her as absent.

It became clear that these tactics were designed to push her into turning to the man who was harassing her. He was the administrative head of the district courts, who held sway over her career. Her fears came true soon enough. One day, she received a call on the landline from the wife of the chief judicial magistrate, inviting her to the ladies sangeet celebrations of the twenty-fifth wedding anniversary of the same judge, scheduled for 10 December 2013. She was told the judge wanted her to 'perform dance on an item song' at the event. Alarmed, she declined, saying she had a prior commitment, but feared her harassment would now double. She had refused a direct invitation from her supervising judge.

She described a broader culture of socializing among judges, which often blurred the lines between professional and personal domains. Parties to mark the retirement or induction of high court judges were routinely attended by all subordinate judges.

For women judges, who had no desire to be there, this posed particular challenges. Ms X recalled that at such events, all women judges of the district court were expected to dress alike, in matching colours, and stand at the entrance offering floral tributes to arriving high court judges.

Public functions are one thing; but treating judges as performers and subordinates is quite another. Despite her earlier refusal, Ms X felt compelled to attend the anniversary celebration the next day, after having refused the judge's request to perform at the previous evening's function. She took her husband and daughter with her, determined to keep her distance from the judge. At one point in the evening, while standing alone with her back turned, the judge came close to her and whispered in her ear that he had 'missed the opportunity of viewing [her] sexy and beautiful figure dancing on the floor'. On another occasion, on 22 February 2014, at the wedding celebrations of a judicial officer, the judge approached her in the presence of her daughter. He ran his hand down Ms X's spine and told her that 'your work is very good, but you are far more beautiful than your work'.[5] Without turning, she took her daughter's hand and left the party.

After the incident, Ms X tried to reach the Chief Justice of the Madhya Pradesh High Court to request an appointment and lodge a complaint. He did not respond. His secretary later denied that she had made any calls. Since the calls had been made from landlines, there was no record to confirm them. On the advice of a senior lawyer, she approached another high court judge, hoping he might intercede on her behalf. At his residence, he asked what the matter was. She replied in Hindi, '*Sir, usne mere saath battameezi ki* (Sir, he misbehaved with me)'. The judge raised his hand and cut her short. '*Bas* (Enough),' he said, seeming to indicate that he was aware of the antecedents of the judge in question and needed no further elaboration. Later, when he appeared before various committees and was asked whether Ms X had ever informed him about the sexual harassment she faced, he admitted that she had come to meet him. But when pressed on whether she had spoken of the harassment, he answered, 'No.' He knew, of course, that he had not allowed her to speak. Male bonding won the day.

Predictably, Ms X was promptly transferred from Gwalior to Sidhi on 8 July 2014. Sidhi was remote, far from both Gwalior and Delhi. At the time, Ms X was living in Gwalior with her two daughters. Her husband worked in Delhi and travelled back each week to be with the family. One of her daughters was in Class 10 at a school with no hostel facility. Under the rule of transfers, a woman judge with a daughter in Class 10 should not be transferred mid-term if the school has no hostel. The rule was ignored. The transfer committee, headed by a senior judge, ordered her posting regardless. She appealed, citing the rule and her daughter's education. Her representation was rejected.

A few days later, she resigned.

All doors to justice had been closed to her. Her resignation was instantly accepted. To free herself from an unbearable situation, she even paid one month's salary to the state in lieu of her notice period. When she was packing up, reporters turned up to ask why she was leaving. She told them it was for the sake of her daughter's education. That, too, was used against her. She was told she hadn't resigned because of sexual harassment, but because she had 'chosen' her daughter over her work.

It was in these circumstances that she wrote, in August 2014, to the CJI and to the President of India, requesting an inquiry into what had happened to her. Like Rupan, she just sought accountability. While still in service, she had tried repeatedly to gain an audience with the Chief Justice of the high court. Each time, she was refused. At that time, there was no internal complaints committee in the high court to deal with allegations of sexual harassment made by judges

What could I do for her, Ms X had asked. For me, her case was an instant recognition of a pattern of abuse. The subordinate relationship between district court judges and high court judges creates a framework within which sexual harassment thrives. Every promotion depends on spotless annual confidential reports. Any adverse comment from the administrative judge can jeopardize a career.

The task was uphill. Ms X had resigned; she had not been sacked. Dismissal can be challenged, since Article 311 of the Constitution offers government servants protection from wrongful termination, provided it can be proven in an inquiry. A resignation, though, is voluntary. Once tendered, it cannot be withdrawn. Still, what Ms X sought was an inquiry into her allegations, which gave me a path to pursue.

When the news broke, the Chief Justice of Madhya Pradesh High Court rushed to set up an inquiry committee, composed of three judges known to be close to the judge she had named. The accused was not suspended, with the justification that the court lacked the power to do so. Nor did he voluntarily step aside during the inquiry. We challenged the committee's composition. Under the Supreme Court's little-known 'in-house procedure', such a committee must include two judges from outside the High Court in question, and one from within. A Supreme Court bench of Justices J.S. Khehar and Arun Mishra upheld our objection and directed the CJI to constitute a proper committee.

The CJI at the time appointed a panel led by Justice D.Y. Chandrachud, then Chief Justice of the Allahabad High Court, along with two other judges. But the committee was a non-starter: evidence was not taken on oath, there was no cross-examination and it concluded that the allegations were unproved. Some token observations were offered, including the suggestion that judges should not celebrate personal occasions with potential litigants. But these were perfunctory. In practice, the culture of socializing, gift-giving and personal proximity between judges and lawyers remained untouched.

Were we back to square one? It seemed like it.

Some time later, I was invited to speak about the case on the lawns of K.T.S. Tulsi's residence. Among those present was the late Sharad Yadav, a Gandhian and veteran politician. After hearing the account, he told me: 'You have picked up an issue that is like the grain of salt Gandhiji picked up, which led to a movement to end British rule. This issue has the potential to do for women what Gandhiji did for the nation.'

I was taken aback by his words. Where the legal process had stalled, perhaps the political process could begin. Maybe the judge could yet be impeached. True to his word, Sharad Yadav became the first signatory to the impeachment motion in the Rajya Sabha. He reached out to women MPs and secured fifty-eight signatures. Hamid Ansari, then vice president of India and chairperson of the Rajya Sabha, admitted the motion on 25 March 2015.

It then fell to the CJI, H.L. Dattu, to appoint a three-member panel under Section 3 of the Judges (Inquiry) Act, 1968. He appointed Justice Vikramjit Sen (Supreme Court), Justice Manjula Chellur (Chief Justice of the Karnataka High Court) and K.K. Venugopal (senior advocate). When Justice Sen retired during the proceedings, he was replaced by Justice R. Banumathi.

Extensive evidence was presented. Ms X stood her ground, detailing the humiliation she had endured. The high court judge denied the allegations. There was even levity over the meaning of 'item number', until it referred to something like Katrina Kaif's performance in the Hindi film song 'Chikni Chameli'—a reference everyone understood.

The magistrate's wife denied having made any such request to Ms X. But we sought a recording of the sangeet ceremony. The footage showed the judge's daughter performing to 'Nagin', a song considered an item number in its time. The aim was simply to show that such performances were part of the judge's personal events, making his earlier request plausible. Colleagues of Ms X gave evidence against her, describing her as a cantankerous neighbor. The district judge said she was 'in the habit' of complaining about the shortages of a peon or a stenographer. The high court judge she had approached for help said she come to him to mediate on her behalf, but when asked, 'Did she complain to you about sexual harassment?' his answer was simply: 'No.' The secretary to the Chief Justice denied having ever received calls from her requesting an appointment.

Then one witness gave the game away. The chair of the transfer committee—a high court judge—was asked to produce his mobile call records. We had sought these records to show calls between him and the accused judge coinciding with the meetings of the transfer committee. The logs showed calls just before and after the meetings where her transfer was discussed, and many more in between. These were brushed off as 'friendly' exchanges between colleagues. But under questioning, the judge admitted that transfer policy allowed a woman judge to remain in place if her daughter was in Class 10 and studying at a day school without hostel facilities.

When asked if he was aware that Ms X's daughter was in exactly that situation, he said no.

He admitted he had not read her application before rejecting it. The file had reached him over a weekend. He had been 'too busy' to read it before deciding against her.

Ms X, meanwhile, recounted how, on the advice of the high court judge she had asked to intercede, she had once sought to meet the accused judge at his residence by prior appointment. Knowing it was unwise to go alone, she had taken her husband along. On learning that her husband had accompanied her, he sent word that he was 'busy' and could not meet. Later, the judge produced his peon as a character witness. He portrayed himself as a devoted son who cared for his elderly parents. The peon testified that he had not seen Ms X or her husband at the residence that day.

For me, it was appalling to watch high court judges lie and obfuscate to protect one of their own. How could I continue to appear before judges who lived such double lives? What respect could I hold for a system that closed ranks against the testimony of a woman judge? Judges must be beyond reproach if the institution is to command public trust. If a high court judge is tainted by moral turpitude, what faith can litigants place in the judiciary?

At the end of the inquiry, I believed we had proved the charges. But when the report was released, the three-member committee hedged. They did not find him guilty of sexual harassment; however, they did not declare him innocent either. They concluded only that the case had not been proved 'beyond reasonable doubt'. Under the Constitution, a judge can only be removed if a committee of three judges makes a finding of misconduct. That report then goes to Parliament, which must vote on the removal. Even then, Parliament may choose not to act. I had seen this before. Years earlier, when I had raised allegations of corruption against Justice V. Ramaswami of the Supreme Court, the committee had found him guilty. The report went to Parliament. But the Congress party, which had appointed him, abstained from the vote. He was not removed.[6]

In Ms X's case, the committee arrived at what I can only call a face-saving compromise. They held that she was entitled, under existing rules, to remain in Gwalior while her daughter was in Class 10, and that her transfer was unlawful. They acknowledged that the transfer had forced her resignation. But they refused to describe the transfer as retaliatory or as victimization for having complained of sexual harassment.

The committee recommended her reinstatement.

But because there was no formal finding of 'misconduct', the report was never placed before Parliament. It remains on record in the Rajya Sabha.

Ms X now had to decide how to proceed. I believed we should challenge the finding that the charge of sexual harassment had not been proved 'beyond reasonable doubt'. The committee had applied the wrong standard of proof. That threshold belongs to criminal law, where a person's liberty is at stake. In matters of judicial conduct and removal from office, the correct standard is the 'balance of probabilities'—a lower threshold. But, by then,

Ms X had lost faith in the system. Fatigue had set in. She wanted to give up, yet could not.

I suggested we file a petition directly in the Supreme Court, treating her resignation as a deemed dismissal, coerced by an unlawful transfer. She agreed. And so we were back in the Supreme Court, this time demanding reinstatement. The judges were relieved to sidestep the question of sexual harassment—too messy, too revealing of the court's culture of male bonding and complicity. Over time, most of the judges who heard the case expressed sympathy for Ms X and referred the matter back to the full court of the Madhya Pradesh High Court, to consider whether her resignation should be treated as withdrawn.

The full court rejected her plea. The Chief Justice conveyed the decision: She had resigned and couldn't now be reinstated. The judges of the Madhya Pradesh High Court had learnt nothing. They closed ranks once more and supported the decision of the former Chief Justice.

That set the stage for us to argue in the Supreme Court against the decision of the Madhya Pradesh High Court, which had acted on the administration's side.

The case was heard by justices L. Nageshwar Rao and B.R. Gavai. I argued that Ms X, as both judge and woman, had been forced to choose between her duty to her daughter's education, and her duty to herself as a working woman. That choice violated her right to work. She should not have been presented with such a choice. She was not seeking back pay for the seven years she had been out of service. She asked only to return to the bench, with her seniority intact. It was the first case of its kind.

In a historic judgment, the court agreed.

The bench held that her right to work had been violated. Her transfer had contravened the judiciary's own policy on subordinate court judges. One judge on the transfer committee had not even read the annexures to her representation. The bench found the transfer arbitrary, irrational and violative of Article 14 of the Constitution. The court ordered her reinstatement.

Ms X returned to the work she loved. In time, her daughter qualified as an architect.

I once asked her what had triggered her decision to fight the case. She said it was her daughter, who gave her the courage: 'Mum, if you cannot stand up for your own rights, how will you stand up for the rights of others?'

Today, Ms X is again a respected judge in Madhya Pradesh. From time to time, I still see her judgments reported in the press.

Did she receive justice? In my view, no. The judges knew she had been sexually harassed but they would not admit it. The inquiry committee knew she had been harassed but lacked the courage to say it in their report. They saw the link between her unlawful transfer and harassment but refused to acknowledge it. Why? To protect the institution. They could not see that the reputation of the institution would be strengthened by holding a guilty man to account. Or that the integrity of the court depends on safe workplaces for women judges. The man in question faced no consequence. He retired with his name intact.

Ask any judge of the Madhya Pradesh High Court from that time, and you may get a knowing smile: 'Oh, that one? The one who got away.' None came forward to attest to his character. The judge who signed her transfer without even reading the file became a Chief Justice of the Delhi High Court. The Chief

Justice who refused to meet her—Justice Khanwilkar—rose to the Supreme Court later. It is my belief that this controversy may have delayed his appointment to the apex court. He now holds post-retirement office as the Lokpal of India.

I continue to represent women who face harassment. The judiciary's dirty secret remains sealed.

For Ms X, reinstatement was vindication enough. She returned to the work she had been forced to leave, her name unblemished. A section of the bar had tried to paint her as rude and abrasive, but the profession welcomed her back as a good and incorruptible judge.

Now, she is a happy woman. Her daughter, whose words had supported her mother while she fought against the odds, smiles in that knowledge. But there is another hopeful afterlife to her story. In a recent conversation, Ms X told me that the culture of sycophancy expected of women judges in the Madhya Pradesh judiciary had changed dramatically since the verdict of her case. No longer were women judges expected to welcome high court judges at appointment or retirement parties with flowers. In fact, there was no compulsion to attend such parties at all. At seminars and conferences, women judges were being treated as intellectual equals. Her professionalism was appreciated by the bench and the bar. To her colleagues, she had become a role model who had successfully fought to bring out a change in the culture of misogyny that existed within the district judiciary. For me, this was compensation enough for five years of labour. It was a vindication of the rule of law.

This is not to say that sexual harassment of women in the judicial system has ended but that the arduous fight against it in this case proved successful.

RM: The question, then, is this: what is justice? Is it the acknowledgement of wrong? Or the retribution that follows?

IJ: The idea of justice in conflict resolution is not the same as justice in the abstract. Conflict exists; the question is how it is to be resolved. That is one of the primary functions of the judiciary. Resolution must offer more than one path, so that the individual who seeks justice can find a form that fits. In cases of workplace harassment, however, there is a non-negotiable minimum: recognition that women are not property and misogyny has no place in law. Once this is accepted, resolution should take the form chosen by the wronged party.

In Ms X's case, there was no such recognition. For me, the matter remains unfinished. For her, reinstatement in the judiciary—the institution she still called home—was justice enough. It acknowledged the gendered coercion that had driven her resignation. Yet any reckoning with justice often carries an expectation of retribution. Speaking for myself, I do not believe that all demands for justice must end in retribution. Nor do I believe criminal law is the only path to justice. Demands often voiced on public platforms, such as calls for death for the accused, do not resonate with me. Civil remedies are frequently ignored and deserve greater exploration. But because they are expensive, requiring exorbitant court fees, they have sadly remained underutilized. In our country, the concept of justice is especially hard to define. The system is plagued by delay. Justice is fought for inch by inch. When the wrongdoer is powerful, the process itself becomes punishment for the victim. In cases of harassment, victims are pursued and discredited; attempts are made to methodically strip away their credibility. With social media, the burden only grows:

the victim becomes the offender, subject to shame, threats and abuse from a faceless crowd. From the outside, all these factors make justice appear illusory.

In the end, it comes down to what the victim seeks. For some, it means ensuring the perpetrator receives punishment in proportion to the harm caused. For others, it means having the harm acknowledged in a court of law as well as in public opinion. In my experience, the women I have represented have often sought the latter. More than anything else, this explains why Ms X chose reinstatement as her form of justice.

5

THE LOST YEARS

RM: I want to ask you about your years with the government as the additional solicitor general, when you were no longer in private practice. What is your retrospective assessment of those years, 2009–2014?

IJ: If you recall, I wrote an article you had published a few years ago, titled 'Outsider Inside'. The title said it all. Nothing in my past had prepared me for the job. My appointment as the additional solicitor general of India was exceptional in many ways, apart from my gender. I was the first woman from the Supreme Court bar to hold the position. I had a known record of work on human rights and, of course, gender justice. I was not a member of the ruling Congress party then, nor am I now. In fact, my background could easily have been seen as being at odds with State power. After all, rights are claimed *against* the State.

So I was as surprised as anyone when the appointment came through. To this day, I don't really know which considerations went into it. I was on a flight from Delhi to Washington DC when I received a call from the Attorney General's office—

personally from the late Goolam E. Vahanvati—asking for my consent to be nominated for the post.

The appointment of an additional solicitor general is made by the Cabinet Committee on Appointments and rests entirely at the government's discretion. There are no rules or criteria for who should be appointed to the ASG position. Vahanvati knew me mainly from across the courtroom, as an opponent in the cases I had argued. He had represented Air India in the matters I took up on behalf of the air hostesses in the 1970s. It was deeply satisfying to learn that my opponents respected my legal acumen enough to trust me with the job, knowing full well my long-standing commitment to human rights and gender justice.

It is important to put on record that law officers are not meant to be mouthpieces for the government they represent in court. Their role is to advise the government on the law, not the other way around. We appear for the government, yes, but that does not mean echoing its views or surrendering our independent judgement. The responsibility is to present the legal position with integrity, rather than mortgage one's mind to the State. Law officers also have the privilege of being consulted on proposed policies and can advise on questions of legality whenever required.

Bearing all this in mind, I agreed to my appointment. There is a well-known articulation of this position which resonates with me—the case of Sally Yates, who served as Acting Attorney General of the United States in 2017. She was asked to implement an executive order of the first Donald Trump-led administration that would have led to the racial profiling of immigrants. Yates refused to do so. She issued a public statement explaining why she believed the order was unlawful:

> My responsibility is to ensure that the position of the Department of Justice is not only legally defensible, but is informed by our best view of what the law is after consideration of the facts. In addition, I am responsible for ensuring that the positions we take in court remain consistent with this institution's solemn obligation to always seek justice and stand for what is right. At present, I am not convinced that the defence of the Executive Order is consistent with these responsibilities nor am I convinced that the Executive Order is lawful.
>
> Consequently, for so long as I am the Acting Attorney General, the Department of Justice will not present arguments in defence of the Executive Order, unless and until I become convinced that it is appropriate to do so.[1]

This is how I saw my job as an additional solicitor general. There were times when I refused to take on cases that, in my view, went against the fundamental rights of people—cases defending 'encounter deaths', for example. Since there were multiple additional solicitors, those cases were simply assigned to someone else. But this is not an institutional solution. There should be room within the system to advise the government when it is acting against the rule of law.

During my tenure, I wrote to the then Prime Minister, Manmohan Singh, demanding removal from office of a former Supreme Court judge—then serving as the head of the West Bengal Human Rights Commission—for alleged acts of sexual harassment against an intern. It was not an easy position to take. Being an insider came with its own burden. The government sought the opinion of another additional solicitor general and concluded that the judge could be removed through due process and that the allegations merited investigation. But no investigation followed. When the judge resigned, I faced fierce opposition from within the bar. Colleagues rushed to defend the retired Supreme Court judge. 'Why isn't the intern filing a criminal prosecution?' they asked. I responded that the choice of remedy was hers alone. The responsibility of the government was to investigate a credible accusation. This was not the only time I had to speak out on allegations of sexual harassment made by interns against former judges of the Supreme Court. My insistence on accountability was seen by some as unbecoming of a law officer. But for me, it was a continuation of my work as a practising lawyer. I saw it as a core duty of any law officer—to protect the rights of women at work.

Among criminal matters, I represented the CBI in prosecuting several police officers implicated in the murders of Sohrabuddin Sheikh and his wife Kauser Bi during the Gujarat riots in 2005. It was alleged that Sheikh was a wanted criminal who had been shot in an encounter while he was on the run. It was the same case in which the then home minister of Gujarat and current union home minister, Amit Shah, was an accused.

I opposed bail for several high-ranking Gujarat police officers. Despite being represented by some of the best lawyers in the country, they did not secure bail. I remember one case in particular, where I opposed bail all the way from the magistrate's court to the Supreme Court. The officer in question arrived at the magistrate's court in an ambulance, accompanied by his astrologer, hoping to secure a favourable decision. The magistrate denied bail. So did the Supreme Court.

I recount this because I believe that this very case later became the basis for my political targeting by the NDA government. In 2016, the FCRA registration[2] of the Lawyers Collective was cancelled on what I believe were false and frivolous grounds.

It was enough to mark me out as an 'enemy' of the ruling party. I resigned as when the 2014 election results were declared, in keeping with the tradition of allowing the incoming government to appoint its own law officers. After that, I returned to private practice and resumed my work in the field of human rights.

I was now free to be my own person. After I returned to my private practice, I was asked to represent Sanjiv Bhatt, a police officer who had alleged that the chief minister of Gujarat during the 2002 riots—now the Prime Minister—had instructed the police to 'go slow'.[3] Bhatt was seeking an impartial inquiry into the allegations against him. The case was heard by Chief Justice H.L. Dattu and Justice Arun Mishra. His request was denied.

I believe my track record, particularly my role in opposing bail for police officers implicated in the Gujarat killings, was never forgotten by the ruling BJP. In time, it became another reason to target me.

Around the same time, I was arguing other politically sensitive cases. Among them was one against Vasundhara Raje, the chief minister of Rajasthan, concerning the Dholpur properties she had acquired as part of her divorce settlement. The hearings drew significant public attention. Soon after, in 2016, we received a communication from the Ministry of Home Affairs stating that the accounts of the Lawyers' Collective were to be investigated.

We later discovered that the complaint prompting the inquiry had originated from an individual connected to the officer on special duty to Vasundhara Raje. The Lawyers' Collective had long held a valid FCRA registration, enabling us to receive international and domestic funding to support our work—particularly with people living with HIV and survivors of domestic violence. Despite years of regular audits and fully compliant financial disclosures, our registration was abruptly cancelled on the vague allegation that our accounts were not properly maintained.

We challenged the cancellation in court for one simple reason: I refused to be victimized. The matter remains pending.

Much later, in 2019, we were taken by surprise when we received notice that a petition against the Lawyers' Collective was to be heard in the Supreme Court on 8 May. It had been filed by an obscure, previously unheard-of NGO called Lawyers' Voice, founded by a self-proclaimed member of the BJP. The organization had no Permanent Account Number card, no funding, no credible public record. The petition demanded that criminal proceedings be initiated against the Lawyers' Collective for alleged violations of Indian criminal law. The petitioner was represented by the then Advocate General of Madhya Pradesh, who has since been appointed a judge.

At the same time, I was continuing my work representing women who had faced sexual harassment. Around that period, a woman employee of the Supreme Court accused the sitting CJI of sexually harassing her. I gave three consecutive interviews on the matter—one each to Rajdeep Sardesai, Karan Thapar and Shereen Bhan, on 5, 6 and 7 May 2019, respectively. On 8 May, the last working day of the Supreme Court before the summer recess, the petition against the Lawyers' Collective was taken up in court by none other than the Chief Justice himself, the very individual facing allegations of sexual harassment. He passed an *ex parte* order, issuing notice on the petition and indicating that investigating agencies could proceed against us.

Weeks later, on 23 June 2019, the Ministry of Home Affairs handed over the case to the CBI. There seemed to be, put mildly, a confluence of interests at work. The FIR registered against me alleged corruption under the Prevention of Corruption Act, 1988, for having accepted foreign funding during my tenure as the ASG, as a 'government servant'. In fact, I had written authorization from the Minister of Law and Justice, Veerappa Moily, permitting me to receive renumeration from the Lawyers' Collection. At the time, the collective's work focused on issues of violence against women, which closely aligned with my legal practice and public advocacy. There was no conflict of interest between this work and the government's stated commitments to gender justice. On the contrary, my work strengthened those goals.

Legally, too, the charge did not hold. As the ASG, I was not a 'government servant' under the Prevention of Corruption Act, and the restrictions under the act did not apply to me. The Chief Justice retired soon after. He was later nominated to the Raja Sabha by the NDA government. The minister, who had been an accused in the Sohrabuddin encounter and was discharged, became free to accept public office and remains the Minister of Home Affairs to this day.

Our investigation continues, and I cannot comment further while the matter is *sub judice*. But I can say that I have experienced the adverse political consequences of the work I did, both as ASG and as a human rights lawyer. There was, unmistakably, a convergence of interests between those who wanted to silence my voice and a ruling party that never forgot my work as ASG. That convergence found expression in the FIR against the Lawyers' Collective, which is still under investigation. I, however, believe that I am not a martyr, nor a victim, nor a hero—just me.

RM: Let me intervene with a question here: you've said that this particular experience, and this action taken against you and the Lawyers' Collective, made you realize that what you had taken for granted as your civil and political rights were, actually, under threat; that you could not assume they were guaranteed. Do you still hold this view?

IJ: Most certainly. If you look at the cyclical phases in my career—and, I think, of many in my generation—you'll see that there was a time when we worked primarily on social and economic rights: the right to health, to minimum wages, to freedom from bonded labour, to food, shelter and a decent environment. There is really no end to what are called the unarticulated social and economic rights embedded in the Constitution of India.

That period marked what I described as an era of democratic lawyering, when we used the Constitution as it was meant to be used, i.e., as an instrument of justice and inclusion. We took our civil and political rights for granted, assuming they could never be taken away. True, during the Emergency they were suspended, but they were later restored through the political process, and we believed such a suspension could not take place again.

Today, those rights are being suspended once again. This time, without any formal amendment to the Constitution. Criminal law had become a tool of persecution rather than prosecution. My friends sometimes ask, 'But why does this shock you? Didn't you expect it?' And my answer is: No, I didn't. When I went to court seeking criminal action where it was necessary but denied, I believed I was upholding the Constitution. The law, then, was on my side. It was during that period I realized the ruling party fears the law because a vigilant judiciary can use it effectively against them. That fear, of the power of the Constitution, will remain, until they succeed in capturing the judiciary ideologically, a process that is already underway. Once that process is complete, there will be nothing left for them to fear. For me, too, my personal perspective shifted to the defence of civil and political rights of others who were being persecuted by the State.

Yet in a strange way, this moment reaffirms my faith in the power of the Constitution. It is this faith that keeps me going. History has once again carved out our role as lawyers: to resist the hijacking of the judiciary by ruling parties, whether through the appointment of judges of their choice or by intimidating judges and lawyers who stand as the frontline defenders of both the judiciary and the Constitution. I consider my time in office as the 'lost years' not because I was later targeted, but because I realized that an outsider to power can never truly become an insider to the very power she has challenged throughout her professional career. My choices were made long before I was appointed ASG and they did not change, leaving me with a five-year hiatus from the path I had always chosen. In retrospect, those years taught me that there is a battle for justice to be fought both inside the court and outside it, both within the State and beyond it.

6

WHO IS A CITIZEN?

RM: You were also involved in the challenge to the Citizenship Amendment Act, 2019. I want you to tell me a little bit about the current status of cases against the Citizenship Amendment Act.

IJ: There are two broad categories of cases currently pending in the courts. The first concerns issues specific to the State of Assam, where there has been an ongoing attempt to create a National Register of Citizens (NRC). Among these is a case decided on challenging a law that enabled the grant of citizenship to migrants from what is now Bangladesh, up to and including March 1971. The second category is the constitutional challenge to the Citizenship Amendment Act, 2019, which is based on the argument that the act provides a fast-track route to Indian citizenship for certain religious groups—Hindus, Sikhs, Buddhists, Jains, Parsis and Christians—from Afghanistan, Bangladesh and Pakistan, while excluding Muslims. These two categories of cases require separate treatment, both in legal argument and historical context.

As of today, there is no nationwide citizenship register in India. However, the Citizenship Act does provide for the creation of such a register, and Assam remains the only state where an NRC has been implemented under Supreme Court supervision. Back in 2015, when the Supreme Court was monitoring the NRC process in Assam, I was approached by several groups concerned about exclusion due to lack of documentation, in particular, people unable to prove ancestry because of migration, displacement or poverty. Since then, I've remained engaged in court cases dealing with citizenship, particularly from Assam. I had always taken my own citizenship for granted. But it became clear that not everyone can.

I am older than the Constitution itself and owe my own citizenship to the founding moment of the republic. My parents migrated to India from what is now Pakistan during Partition. I am a citizen by birth—but in today's India, being born here does not necessarily entitle you to citizenship. The law has changed. Now, even birth in India doesn't automatically confer citizenship. And those who live along the eastern border, where historic back-and-forth migration has occurred for decades, face the possibility not just of being denied citizenship, but even the right to reside in the country they call home.

To understand how we arrived here, we must begin with the Citizenship Act of 1955, and the context of Partition. Partition created two nations—India and Pakistan—and sparked one of the largest mass migrations and forced displacements in human history. Millions crossed the newly drawn borders. The scars of that migration are visible in both the Constitution and the Citizenship Act of 1955, in that the Constitution enabled migrating back and forth at least until 1948.

The Constitution, particularly Article 5, refers to citizenship at the 'commencement of the Constitution'. It conferred citizenship on persons who were domiciled in the 'territory of India' at that time. Notably, it did not refer to 'undivided India'. That meant individuals who were domiciled in what became Pakistan were excluded unless they migrated back and met certain conditions. So, from the very outset, the Constitution required people of undivided India to choose where they would live and gain citizenship.

On the western border, this decision-making was immediate, shaped by the violence and trauma of Partition. But on the eastern border, the movement continued for decades. The borders were not physically secure, nor was there a legal permit system in place in 1947.

Article 6 of the Citizenship Act, 1955 carried forward the legacy of Partition by specifically addressing the status of persons who migrated into the 'territory of India' from the 'territory now included in Pakistan'.[1] It acknowledged that the question of citizenship could not be resolved solely by a fixed date or geographic line as it would continue to bear the imprint of historical upheaval. This citizenship was subject to two conditions: (a) the person's parents or any one grandparent had to have been born in 'undivided' India, i.e., India as defined in the Government of India Act, 1935; and (b) (i) where such person has so migrated before 19 July 1948, such a person must have been ordinarily resident in the territory of India from the date of his/her migration; or (ii) where such person has so migrated on or after 19 July 1948, and has been registered as a citizen of India by an officer appointed in that behalf by the Government of the

Dominion of India, on an application made to such an officer before the commencement of the Constitution.

Under Article 7, anyone who migrated from the territory of India to the territory of Pakistan after 1 March 1947 would not be considered a citizen of India. However, this exclusion was subject to an important proviso: citizenship could still be conferred if such a person returned to the territory of India under a 'permit of permanent return or resettlement' issued by the Government of India.[2] Anyone returning under such a 'permit' would be deemed to have migrated to the territory of India after 19 July 1948, as envisaged under Article 6.

The founding moment of our nation, deeply embedded in an age of migration, is reflected in this proviso. It recognized the possibility of return for those who had left India, under the authority of a law that permitted permanent return or resettlement. In doing so, it kept the proverbial door open for persons of Indian origin from undivided India.

RM: Surely, the Constituent Assembly debated a proviso of such far-reaching implications?

IJ: Yes, it did. But as you can see, citizenship continues to be a contested issue even today. The very basis on which citizenship was once acquired—birth—has since all but disappeared. At the time of drafting of the Constitution, one of the core questions being debated was how to address the back-and-forth movement of people during the Partition. The issue resurfaced again in reference to Assam in 1971, during the Bangladesh Liberation War, when large-scale migration occurred across the eastern border.

While explaining the draft Article 5AA (later Article 7), Dr B.R. Ambedkar began with the caveat that he was not as fully versed in the administrative aspects as the ministers who were directly handling the matter. He clarified that the drafting committee's intention was this:

> If a person who has migrated to Pakistan and, after having gone there, has returned to India on the basis of a permit which was given to him by the Government of India not merely to enter India, but a permit which will entitle him to resettlement or permanent return, it is only such person who will be entitled to become a citizen of India on the commencement of this Constitution.[3]

Dr Ambedkar went on to explain why the date of 19 July 1948 had been introduced. By then, the Government of India had shifted its focus to individuals who had left for Pakistan but later sought to return to India to settle permanently under the 'permit system', which came into force on 19 July 1948. However, this system, formally titled 'The Influx from West Pakistan (Control) Ordinance, 1948', applied only to the western border.[4]

The situation on the eastern border was different. Responding in the Constituent Assembly, N. Gopalaswamy Ayyangar, the minister in charge, observed that migration of Muslims from East Bengal was 'nothing new' and, therefore, introducing a permit system similar to the one for West Pakistan would be inadvisable. Instead, he suggested exploring other methods to control 'the influx of a large number of Muslims from East Bengal to Assam'.[5]

The annual report of the Ministry of External Affairs for 1952–53 further clarified the situation: until 15 October 1952, movement between East Pakistan and the Indian states of Assam and West Bengal on the eastern frontier remained free. This report observed that '[i]n April 1952, Pakistan decided to replace the Permit System between India and West Pakistan by a Passport-cum-Visa System, and also to apply that system to travel between East Pakistan and India, which had hitherto been free'.[6] Migration to and from Assam and East Pakistan, therefore, was an established fact of life. The framers of the Constitution were aware of, and alive to, this fluid movement across the eastern border and that it would require a specific legal framework. This is the reason why there has been movement of persons on the Eastern Border freely without hindrance over the years.

In the meantime, the Citizenship Act of 1955 was enacted, outlining the modes by which citizenship could be acquired. Section 3 of the act provides for citizenship by birth, recognizing every person born in India as an Indian citizen. Over time, this provision was amended—in 1987 and again in 2004—narrowing the scope of citizenship by birth. The law now provides that every person born in India between the commencement of the Constitution and 1 July 1987 is a citizen. Those born on or after 1 July 1987 but before 3 December 2004 must have at least one parent who was an Indian citizen at the time of birth. For those born on or after 3 December 2004, both parents must be Indian citizens, or one must be a citizen and the other not an illegal migrant, for the child to qualify as a citizen. With effect from July 1987, therefore, India moved away from the very idea of unconditional citizenship by birth. Section 4 of the act provides for citizenship by descent for persons born outside India; Section 5 for citizenship by registration; and Section 6 for citizenship by naturalization.

RM: The eastern border would have come up for consideration again after 1971, wouldn't it?

IJ: Yes, Section 6A of the act was introduced in the context of the Bangladesh Liberation War, which caused large-scale migrations from erstwhile East Pakistan into Assam. This, in turn, sparked an agitation led by sections of students in Assam, most prominently the All Assam Students' Union, who viewed the migrants—many of whom were Bengali-speaking—as a threat to local identity and resources. The unrest was eventually resolved through the Assam Accord, brokered in 1985 by Prime Minister Rajiv Gandhi. This accord led to the Citizenship (Amendment) Act of 1985, which inserted Section 6A into the Citizenship Act of 1955. The new section gave legislative effect to the Assam Accord, granting citizenship to those who had entered India through Assam before the cut-off date of 24 March 1971.

It thus acknowledged them as persons of Indian origin from East Pakistan before that date and deemed them citizens of India.

The provision was later challenged by groups in Assam who identified themselves as 'indigenous'. They argued that granting citizenship to migrants who arrived up to March 1971 would alter the state's demographics and dilute their 'indigenous' identity.

After the creation of Bangladesh, the new nation recognized as citizens only those present within its territory on or before 25 March 1971. Had India not granted citizenship to those who migrated from East Pakistan to India, up to and including 24 March 1971, these individuals would have been rendered stateless.

So, while the Constitution deemed only those who migrated from Pakistan before 19 July 1948 to be Indian citizens, in the case of Assam this cut-off was shifted to March 1971. To me, this is deeply significant, because it reveals the impracticality of fixing 1948 as a permanent boundary in time. Political and personal circumstances can lead to migration across borders at any time, especially where communities share close cultural or linguistic ties. Even the Constituent Assembly realized this fluidity. Dr Ambedkar repeatedly stated that Part II of the Constitution was meant merely as an ad hoc arrangement for the acquisition of citizenship at the commencement of the Constitution. It was never intended to lay down, then or now, who a citizen is. That responsibility was left to Parliament. But even the Citizenship Act of 1955 does not define a 'citizen'. It merely sets out the conditions for acquiring citizenship.

Section 6A, introduced in 1985, recognizes that 'persons of Indian origin' who entered Assam before 1971 would be granted citizenship. This provision was later challenged on the ground that it damaged the rights of the 'indigenous communities' of Assam, though it could not clearly define who the indigenous people of Assam were.

This addition of Section 6A to the Citizenship Act was challenged in the Supreme Court. The Constitution of India makes no reference to 'indigenous people'. What it does recognize are Scheduled Tribes, and it provides special protections for them through the designation of Scheduled Areas, where their customs and systems of local administration are safeguarded.

More importantly, it needs pointing out that Section 6A makes no reference to the religion of migrants. Yet the demand from certain groups was that no one who arrived after 1948 should be granted citizenship.

I was approached by minority rights organizations in Assam to represent migrants or 'persons of Indian origin', who had settled in the state and acquired citizenship by 1971, to defend their position before the Constitution bench of the Supreme Court. It was in that context that I told the court we were dealing with the 'birthmarks of Partition', because migration did not end in 1947. It has been a continuous process, and one could reasonably question why it should end at 1971.

It did not surprise me that the Union of India defended the law in court through its Solicitor General and Attorney General, arguing that it lay within Parliament's plenary power to determine who should be a citizen and who should not. Ironically the same argument could be used to defend the Citizenship (Amendment) Act of 2019, which was already under challenge when the Assam case was being argued.

Our identity, I believe, is best captured in the words of the Supreme Court in the T.M.A. Pai Foundation case, which described India as a 'mosaic' made up of more than a billion tiles, each representing a distinct identity, held together by a common commitment to the values enshrined in the Constitution of India.[7]

This nuance, the distinction between laws that govern the acquisition of citizenship and a broader national identity rooted in our constitutional ethos is almost entirely missing from our public conversation in India. This has led to a situation where attempts are being made to link the grant of citizenship to religious identity rather than fidelity to the values enshrined in the Preamble, which has not been the case at any point of time in Indian's Constitutional history. As early as 1963, in *State Trading*

Corporation of India Ltd. vs Commercial Tax Officer, a nine-judge bench of the Supreme Court acknowledged this absence of a clear definition of Indian citizenship. The case itself dealt with whether a corporation could claim fundamental rights available only to citizens. During the arguments, the then Attorney General for India, M.C. Setalvad, raised the issue of defining citizenship, and the bench took note of it.

Chief Justice B.P. Sinha briefly addressed the point, observing that neither the Constitution nor the Citizenship Act of 1955 had meaningfully defined Indian citizenship. He concluded, however, that it was unnecessary to decide whether Indian citizens existed before the commencement of the Constitution in the context of that particular case.

Justice Hidayatullah, in his concurring opinion, took a broader view. He traced the evolution of the idea of citizenship, from the Greeks and Romans to its modern expressions in American and British thought, and sought to locate its meaning within the Indian Constitution itself. He turned to the Preamble:

> The Preamble in solemn words sums up what is later provided in the Constitution. 'Citizens' in the Preamble mean those individuals who under the Constitution are guaranteed civic rights in the body politic that is India and who can hold public offices and elect their representatives to the Parliament and Assemblies of the people.[8]

He went on to observe that while the Constitution extends certain rights and protections to non-citizens, the Preamble remains a guarantee meant exclusively for citizens. It must be noted that these is no reference of fidelity to a particular religion here in the Preamble.

RM: How does everything you've said so far pertain to the Citizenship (Amendment) Act of 2019?

IJ: The problem with the Citizenship (Amendment) Act, 2019, lies in its attempt to undo long-standing social and political values while at the same time introducing religion as a criterion for citizenship. The contrast becomes clear when you compare Section 6A—in relation to the state of Assam, which recognizes the grant of citizenship to 'persons of Indian origin', and Section 6B—added through the 2019 amendment—which uses the same phrase but expressly excludes Muslims from its scope.

If the idea of the law was to provide citizenship to those who are persecuted in the subcontinent as claimed by the government, the CAA could have simply stated that persons of Indian origin from undivided India persecuted in Pakistan, Bangladesh or Afghanistan or Sri Lanka would be entitled to fast-track citizenship in India. Instead, it obliterates the idea of shared heritage and common affinity by using language that solely excludes Muslims. The act further exempts this religion-based category from two basic legal requirements for entering India: a) that one must enter the country from a valid port of entry; and b) that one must possess valid travel documents. When these conditions are waived, it becomes clear that the law's purpose is not to address persecution, but to create a framework that explicitly excludes Muslims. It removes the stigma of illegality from all illegal migrants except Muslims. This is not the India we chose to build at the time when the Constitution of India came into force .

The CAA seeks to promote an idea of the nation that refuses to acknowledge Muslims as part of 'our own'. If the real intent were to protect those facing persecution in neighbouring countries, there would be no reason for such selective language. As Justice Surya Kant observed in the recent decision upholding the validity of Section 6A the Constitution's idea of fraternity in India is distinct from the European notion.[9] The judgment's most crucial insight is that fraternity cannot be interpreted in a restrictive sense and allow people to choose who their neighbours are.

This, to me, is the very essence of India: an idea that embraces all its people, not just within the boundaries of the republic, but within the values embedded in the Preamble. When I say the Constitution is my home, I mean it in the deepest sense. It gives me identity, comfort and reassurance, because it acknowledges our shared past, our migrations, our comings and goings, our multiple homes and our common origin.

There is no state called Sindh in India anymore, yet I still feel an affinity to it. This is an affinity the Constitution allows me to claim. It is an emotional and historical connection that binds me to my fellow citizens. As a person who has crossed from one part of the continent to another, I feel an enduring sense of belonging not for territorial or linguist reasons but for the framework I inherited from the Constitution, which was my legacy.

I am comforted by the fact that our Constituent Assembly did not think along the lines of those who passed the CAA in 2019. One can only imagine the heightened sense of division at the time when, within just a few years of Partition, the provisions in Part II were being debated—provisions that uniquely included those who had migrated from Pakistan, or even left India and later returned to resettle. And make no mistake, when the Drafting Committee debated this, these ideas were not universally accepted. Some members of the Constituent Assembly strongly opposed granting citizenship to anyone who had remigrated from Pakistan after 15 August 1947. They derided the proposal as 'cheap citizenship' and accused Nehru of appeasing Pakistan and Muslims. Their demand was for stricter, more exclusionary citizenship clauses.

Nehru's reply to these charges was clear:

> I want to know clearly what that word (appeasement) means. Do the honourable members who talk of appeasement think that some kind of rule should be applied when dealing with these people, which has nothing to do with justice or equity? I want a clear answer to that. If so, I would only plead for appeasement. This Government will not go by a hairsbreadth to the right or to left from what they consider to be the right way of dealing with the situation, justice to the individual or the group.[10]

This is the unique nature of our Constitution, and this is the choice we made: not to turn away from the facts of life, from Partition or from our shared heritage. In the same debate, Nehru urged the members to consider that refusing citizenship to those who had once gone to Pakistan but later wished to return to India would violate every canon of justice and equity. One has to understand that clearly.

For me, the right to reside in India for anyone from the subcontinent must be acknowledged, because the birthmarks of Partition are still with us. Migration and residence are phenomena distinct from immigration and citizenship, and the two should not be conflated. To confuse them is to risk the demonization of persons of Indian origin, simply because they have moved across borders, often for reasons beyond their control. Ironically, there is currently a petition pending before the Supreme Court of India seeking recognition of dual citizenship. The argument is that the Constitution contains no express bar on acquiring citizenship of another country alongside Indian citizenship. My reference to the birthmarks of Partition was intended to convey this: Migration back and forth between the two neighbouring countries is the inevitable consequence of partition. Our shared ancestry compels it.

7

THE CONSTITUTION IS MY HOME

RM: You have often spoken about being a refugee and have introduced two very important notions: One, that almost everybody who is a refugee carries what you call the 'birthmarks of Partition'; second, that as a Sindhi, you feel you have neither a state nor a home. Following on from this is your very powerful statement that the Constitution is your home, could you speak about both?

IJ: The first thing I need to point out is that my parents never spoke about the violence they had witnessed during Partition. I have never understood why. Perhaps they wanted to spare us the legacy of violence. Yet, the birthmarks of Partition on them were evident to me: they would not allow us to have Muslim friends. I remember I could not bring the Muslim children in my class home. For me, it was both a contradiction and a challenge.

I realized that my parents had been deeply scared by the violence they saw and the separation they had experienced from home and hearth, yet they would not talk about it. At the same time, they chose to live in a form of apartheid. This was not my way of life. I did not consider the religion of my friends before making them my own. Nevertheless, I carried the feeling of being a refugee. I felt deprived of something, or at least the memory of it, since it was never discussed at home. I began to attribute many of my choices to this rootlessness I had experienced growing up in partitioned India—a rootlessness that has stayed with me. It is almost as if you have no ancestors; you left them behind in Pakistan. Ancestors give you a sense of continuity, which is missing from my life. I have learnt to live with that absence.

This feeling of being a refugee never left me. It carried the quiet conviction that I must, one day, go back to visit Pakistan, to see the house in Karachi where my grandparents once lived. It has always been an unfinished story. I went to Karachi once, but not as a visit to the ancestral home. I didn't see the house my maternal grandparents left behind. That desire remains since I have a distinct memory of it. Even now, I can see it in my mind: one day I will see the house they lived in. I remember it. A bungalow, with an anganwadi. That one visit in my adult years showed me what I was missing. For the first time, I heard Sindhi spoken as the language of governance by immigration officials, at customs, by the police. It came as a shock. We spoke Sindhi at home, but I had never heard it in the public domain. I realized this mattered to me, personally and politically. It felt like home, but it was not. Home was back in India. I may not be one of the founding mothers of the Constitution, but I am one of its founding daughters. Founding a nation is not a moment in time. It is a continuous process, without end. This is where I have lived, loved and worked. This is where home is. The Constitution of

India is not just a text; it's normative in content, and that is where my home lies.

RM: You have said that you have no identifiable place to belong to.

IJ: In India, as a territorial unit, all states are divided along linguistic lines. There is no state or territory defined as Sindh. When people ask me where I am from, the first question almost everyone asks, I cannot name a state in response. I am a Sindhi, born and brought up in Maharashtra. But Marathi is not my mother tongue, so I am not one of them. In a way, this made my migration from Bombay to Delhi easier. Not because Delhi is home—it isn't—but because I have no state to call my own. It was not a difficult decision; I did not feel I was leaving anything behind, except my family. I do not think of Delhi as home, nor do I believe a place becomes your home just because you live there. That requires a profound sense of belonging. When I say I am home, I mean I am comfortable with the covenant I made with the Constitution of India.

RM: So, the Constitution being your home is not just legally speaking, but ...

IJ: I have come to see that there is one thing, and one thing alone, to which I owe my existence: the provision in the Constitution of India that says there shall be no discrimination on the basis of sex.

I have faced discrimination for much of my career in the legal profession. The question, then, is: what enabled me to persist and succeed despite it? My answer always leads back to the single document I have held in court every day of my life. The Constitution of India is not just a text that serves the client or case at hand. In the three cases of sexual harassment I have dealt with, in matters involving the homeless and in the fight for hawkers' rights—not one has been argued without invoking the Constitution and the rights it confers on every citizen.

I began to see my ability to navigate the courts as linked to the fact that I am a woman at work. Article 15 of the Constitution says there shall be no discrimination based on sex. I may be an outsider to the courts, a first-generation lawyer, I may be the wrong sex, but I had to be accepted thanks to Article 15 of the Constitution of India. My acceptance by woman clients and from working-class clients left the courts with no option but to accept me as a professional in court, not just see me as a woman whose place was in the home. That is how I have been able to enter a court with confidence. I once suggested to a young woman legal journalist who was hesitant in her gait, 'Walk as if you owned the court.' This is how I approach the courtroom. This ties in with my belief that the law is both the shield and the sword in your daily life; there is no question of its being one without the other. This is not to say there is no discrimination based on sex in your professional and personal life; there is, but you have the tools to deal with it. Conformism and subordination are still demanded by judges and by male colleagues; they don't let go of that. They cannot abide a woman with a mind of her own, who doesn't toe the line, who speaks plainly. It is not enough to be polite in court; you must also not speak your mind. If you do, you are an 'aggressive' outsider.

RM: Obviously, that is critical in your life as a lawyer, but when you say, 'The Constitution is my home', it carries a much larger sense of belonging ...

IJ: Yes, because the Constitution embodies something greater: an aspiration, certain overarching ideas; it carries the sense of belonging to the values known as the idea of India, territory and values overlap here and you feel at home. You may not have a territorial unit to call your own, but you have an idea to call your own, in common with a community of others who have the same idea never feel alienated: instead, there is a deep solidarity with fellow citizens. That is the essence of citizenship, and what it truly means. That is the norm I identify with, the one into which I was born.

RM: How personal has this relationship with the Constitution been for you?

IJ: The knowledge that I had rights liberated me from the strictures of a conservative family. As refugees from Sindh, our family heirlooms were left behind. It is hardly surprising, then, that when I became a lawyer, it was that 'other side of independence' that drew me in. I was inspired by the fight for social emancipation and, in the words of Justice D.Y. Chandrachud, by 'a fight for undoing historical injustices and for righting fundamental wrongs with fundamental rights'.[1] I belong to a generation in danger of extinction, in mortal terms as well as ideological ones. As a young lawyer, I found my compass in the Directive Principles of State Policy, described as fundamental to the governance of the country.[2] Rights are guaranteed by the Constitution, but they are merely the raw material of one's craft; the real struggle lies in making sure they are implemented and enforced. These include social and economic rights, as well as political and civil and, in practice, they are exercised together. Under international law, civil and political rights, including the guarantee of non-discrimination on grounds of race, caste, religion and sex, are considered immediately enforceable. Economic, social and cultural rights, by contrast, are to be realized progressively. Perhaps it is for this reason that, as lawyers, we have come to take our civil and political rights for granted.

In 1973, the Supreme Court evolved the doctrine of the Constitution's basic features, holding that certain foundational principles cannot be amended. It is a doctrine of self-preservation, intended to safeguard the liberal and secular features of the constitution. All of us need a strategy of self-preservation. For me, it is the Constitution of India that helps me preserve my integrity as a person.

Yet, today, we are witnessing a de facto attack on those very features. India is said to be engaged in a movement to 'decolonize', an impulse that we are told began in 2014. This avowedly ahistorical view is advanced by a Hindu nationalist party that came to power with the aim of establishing a majoritarian Hindu Rashtra.[3] Liberalism as a political philosophy is rejected and secularism supplanted by theocratic impulses The implications are grave for those who believe that democracy, secularism and federalism form basic features of the Constitution and that they constitute the chhatra-chhaaya—the protective canopy—under which they stand.

RM: Do you see this as primarily ideological, or as politically instrumentalist?

IJ: It is both. It is ideological in that it rejects liberalism as the basis of our Constitution. It is instrumentalist in that it mobilizes votes from the majority Hindu community in order to stay in power. Decolonization becomes a proxy for abandoning the Constitution. Hindutva presents itself as a political manifestation of Hinduism and serves as a proxy for the Hindu Rashtra, justified as a way of life rather than as a religion.[4] The consequence is a shift in allegiance, away from the Constitution and towards an appeal to 'culture' as justification for State action. In that shift lies the erosion of fundamental rights. Culture, rather than the Constitution, becomes the touchstone against which the validity of State action is judged. If our courts lend legitimacy to this mode of reasoning, according primacy to cultural nationalism, the one avenue of recourse against majoritarian rule that the Constitution provides may well be lost.

We must ask ourselves how we arrived at this point without any substantial amendment to the Constitution's provisions on secularism and fundamental rights. The answer perhaps is concealed in a more insidious development. The Constitution is simply ignored in governance, leading to its de facto repudiation. In the past, the Constitution of India has undergone frequent amendments, yet its 'basic features' have always been respected. Under what I call the second transformation of the Indian state, when liberalism as an ideology is rejected, there is no need to amend the Constitution. It can just be disregarded. The basic structure has not been removed, but it has been rendered invisible. This is why the second transformation is more dangerous than the first, the Emergency. An emergency, by definition, is temporary. The politics of Hindutva have continued for over a decade and can no longer be described as temporary. They are also likely to prove more difficult to dismantle than the Emergency.

Save for two significant amendments, one abrogating Article 370[5] and the other introducing reservations for economically weaker sections[6] to the exclusion of all other castes, the Constitution itself has stayed intact. The abolition of Article 370 was carried out in August 2019 through a combination of presidential orders and parliamentary legislation, which rendered inoperative the provision granting special constitutional status to the State of Jammu and Kashmir. This was followed by the enactment of the Jammu and Kashmir Reorganisation Act, 2019, which bifurcated the state and converted it into two Union Territories: Jammu and Kashmir, and Ladakh. It effectively redrew the map of India, converting a state into a union territory.

Reservations for economically weaker sections were introduced through the Constitution (103rd Amendment) Act, 2019, which inserted Articles 15(6) and 16(6). This amendment enabled the State to provide reservations in education and public employment for economically weaker sections among citizens not covered by existing reservations for Scheduled Castes, Scheduled Tribes and Other Backward Classes.

Apart from these changes, religion-based distinctions in the grant of citizenship were advanced through executive notifications issued under the Foreigners Act, 1946, a colonial statute enacted to regulate the entry, stay, and exit of foreigners; the Passports Act, 1967; and eventually through an amendment to the Citizenship Act, 1955. This approach was later codified through the Citizenship (Amendment) Act, 2019, which amended the Citizenship Act, 1955, to provide a fast-track route to citizenship for specified religious minorities from Pakistan, Bangladesh and Afghanistan. That amendment relied on Article 11 of the Constitution, which empowers the Parliament to legislate on matters of citizenship.[7]

These measures have been challenged before the Supreme Court, which will ultimately have to determine whether they violate the basic features of the Constitution and the principle of secularism that it enshrines.

RM: Do you see a real danger of its basic structure being tampered with?

IJ: Yes. The de facto abandonment of liberalism amounts to an abandonment of the Constitution's basic structure. To understand how we arrived here, and what is unfolding now, we must revisit the history of constitutional subversions over the past seventy-five years. There have been at least two major distortions of the constitutional order, with a third currently underway.

The Emergency of 1975 was the first profound shock to the liberal framework of the Constitution. The legitimacy of protest, inherited from the freedom movement and grounded in traditions of non-violent struggle and civil disobedience, was brought to an abrupt halt when the Emergency was proclaimed in June 1975. For the first time, the Indian state shifted from being anchored in the principles of liberal democracy, shaped by universal ideals as well as India's own historical experience, to a concentration of power in the executive, vested with sweeping authority to proclaim a state of internal emergency and suspend the right to life.

Are we witnessing something similar today? In terms of the denial of civil and political rights, there are parallels. As a constitutional phenomenon, however, the present moment differs markedly from the Emergency of 1975. The defining feature of the Emergency was that the transformation of the State occurred through the Constitution itself, under Article 352. It may be argued that the departure from liberal democracy was effected by constitutional means. When *habeas corpus* petitions were filed challenging unlawful detentions, the Supreme Court, in its majority opinion in the *ADM Jabalpur vs Shivkant Shukla* case,[8] which we've brought up earlier, held that right to life could be suspended during an Emergency. Justice H.R. Khanna's dissent, affirming that the right to life could not be suspended even in such circumstances, remains a moral and constitutional touchstone for those who value liberty.

The Emergency was met with widespread protest and was eventually withdrawn in accordance with law. Elections followed, and the ruling party was voted out of office. The succeeding government amended the Constitution to remove the power to declare an 'internal emergency', again through constitutional processes. Throughout the Emergency and its aftermath, the Constitution remained at the centre of India's political life.

RM: What exactly do you mean by the second transformation of the Indian state?

IJ: You see, if the Emergency represented the 'first transformation', what we are witnessing now is the second, one that is of a different kind. Many authors and activists describe the present moment as an 'undeclared Emergency'.[9] The phrase captures only part of the reality. The Emergency of the 1970s did not repudiate the legitimacy of liberal democracy. By contrast, the present ruling party makes little effort to defend it.

The Rashtriya Swayamsevak Sangh and the BJP, together with their wide network of affiliated organizations, have stated their objective of reshaping India into a Hindu state. They seek to recast history by claiming that ancient India was inherently liberal and democratic, and that a seamless continuity exists between that past and the constitutional present. Mughal rule and British colonialism are portrayed as aberrations, interruptions in an otherwise civilizational arc, with true decolonization requiring a return to an imagined ancient order. This narrative is historically false and represents a rejection of liberalism as it is understood today and as it is embedded in the Constitution. Concepts such as due process and the independence of the judiciary were introduced during the colonial period. The rule of law, as preserved in the Constitution of India, does not derive from ancient practice. It reflects in significant measure continuity with a British legal tradition that has since assumed near-universal form.

To advance this project, legal as well as extra-legal strategies have been deployed. The BJP rejects the core values of the Constitution. The effort is directed towards transforming the state so that it is governed less by constitutional principle than by an ideology of 'cultural nationalism', with 'culture' defined by a cynical form of Hindutva politics.

In effect, the ruling party is transforming the nature of the State from a liberal and secular republic into a Hindu nationalist one. This shift has occurred without any formal amendment to the Constitution. Its normative content is set aside, and actions that run contrary to constitutional principle are justified in the name of allegiance to an ancient culture, now reframed as a project of decolonization. This is what I mean when I say that the State has elevated a norm above the Constitution of India, a standard against which the legality of State action is to be judged. It asserts that there exists something more fundamental than the Constitution's own basic structure, a higher source of authority to which allegiance must be owed and by which accountability is to be measured. This is a subtle device. It allows the Constitution to be circumvented without formal repeal and without any apparent breach of fidelity, while simultaneously eroding accountability to Parliament. Such a shift, however, depends upon a prior weakening of other mechanisms of restraint. The separation of powers between the executive, legislature and judiciary must be diluted. The independence of the media must be compromised. Civil society, particularly when it is vocal and critical, must be marginalized or silenced. It is in that sense that we are confronting more than an 'undeclared emergency'. What is at stake is a repudiation of liberalism itself and its attempted replacement with Hindu nationalism, or what is described as cultural nationalism.

Its essential element is the rejection of the Constitution as a whole and, in practice, the rejection of the rule of law. This helps explain the repeated invocation of the supposed divine origin or destiny of political leaders, a rhetorical shift away from the idea of democratically elected representatives towards a conception of authority grounded in divine sanction.

A precondition for this transformation is the compromising of the independence and institutional integrity of all organs of governance. Once that occurs, the checks and balances that restrain electoral power fall away, leaving dominance without effective accountability. This is no longer speculative; it has already happened. Consider the executive. The Janata Party once enforced a rule that no member could belong simultaneously to another organization, which made it impossible for an RSS member to serve in government. No such restriction exists today, whether within the RSS or the BJP. It is worth recalling that the ban on the RSS was lifted largely on its assurance that it functioned as a cultural rather than a political organization. By 2020, of the fifty-three BJP ministers in the then Narendra Modi-led government, thirty-eight were reported to have an RSS background.[10] Even during the oath-taking of MPs, chants of 'Jai Shri Ram!' were used to heckle Muslim MPs.

Every organ of the State now carries a significant presence of RSS ideologues who advance its agenda from within. Tathagata Roy, an RSS ideologue and then governor of Meghalaya, once tweeted in support of an (unnamed) retired army officer's suggestion that Kashmir and Kashmiris be economically boycotted.[11] Here was a constitutional functionary, sworn to uphold the Constitution, appearing to endorse discrimination against fellow citizens on the basis of ethnicity and religion.

Consider Parliament. A common response to searching questions is that there is 'no data available'. One is left to ask whether policymaking is proceeding without an evidentiary foundation. Functions once undertaken by the IAS are increasingly channelled through the NITI Aayog, which in turn collaborates with selected NGOs and consultants prepared to operate within the government's narrowing conception of constitutional liberty. Over the past decade, there has been a steady erosion of Parliament's deliberative authority. Contentious legislation has been introduced or sustained through ordinances, thereby curtailing debate and scrutiny, as in the ordinance concerning control over services in the Delhi government.

RM: I want to return to the point you made about there being a norm above the norm—can you elaborate on what exactly you meant by that?

IJ: The Indian Constitution marked a decisive rupture with the country's social, cultural and political past. For the first time, it enshrined values such as equality, democracy, secularism and the dignity of the individual, principles that had no secure place in ancient India. These were not inherited certainties but hard-won achievements of the freedom movement and the anti-colonial struggle, given enduring form in the Constitution under the stewardship of Dr Ambedkar.

There was a conscious effort to de-Brahminize Indian society and to dismantle the caste hierarchy through a written Constitution that guaranteed equality of status and opportunity. In 1947, India ceased to be a colony and, through the exercise of self-determination, became a republic. What emerged was a successor state that was *sui generis*. We inscribed our future upon what was, in constitutional terms, a clean slate.

No successor state is bound by the laws, customs or practices of its predecessor except by choice. Independence from colonial rule did not arrive as a mere administrative transfer of authority. It followed a sustained political struggle that began with the freedom movement and culminated in the drafting of a self-conscious Constitution. Transformations in statehood may occur through revolution, annexation, cession or secession.

What do I mean by this? What occurred in India was, in a sense, revolutionary. Revolutions are marked by a shift in sovereignty. The Indian Independence Act 1947 transferred power to the Constituent Assembly, granting it the authority to shape the new state as it saw fit. The princely states were integrated into this emerging Union. The Constituent Assembly declared that sovereignty resided in the people of India, a symbolic and juridical affirmation of the transfer of sovereign power.

It was in this moment that fundamental rights were conferred upon the people. An independent judiciary was established, vested with the authority to strike down any law, whether pre-existing or newly enacted, if it contravened those rights. Article 395 formally repealed the Indian Independence Act 1947. Its purpose had been fulfilled, and with that repeal, the legal continuity of colonial rule was brought to an end.

While it is true that the Indian Constitution adopted certain structural features from the Government of India Act, 1935, including aspects of the federal framework, the distribution of powers between the Centre and the states, the office of governor and bicameral legislatures, it does not follow that the Constitution is a mere replica of that statute. The incorporation of fundamental rights and the conferment of judicial review fundamentally altered the character of the earlier imperial framework. The Constituent Assembly drafted a republican charter. It was not a colonial blueprint. In framing it, the assembly drew upon global constitutional practices developed in liberal democracies, adapting them to India's own conditions and aspirations. India was not simply inherited from the British; a new nation came into being. It was recognized internationally and admitted to the United Nations as a member in its own right. It is therefore misleading to suggest, as some on the right have done, that there is an unbroken continuity of political and philosophical thought between ancient India and the Constitution. India as a modern nation has its own origin story. It is not the outcome of a gradual evolution of ideas from antiquity, but the result of a conscious constitutional founding.

The successor state determines what it will retain and what it will discard from the past. That is precisely what India did in 1950. Article 13 makes this explicit. It provides that all laws in force within the territory of India shall be void to the extent that they are inconsistent with fundamental rights. The term 'law' is defined broadly to include rules, regulations, customs and usages that have the force of law. Under the common law tradition, a custom acquires legal authority if it can be shown to have existed since 'time immemorial'. At Independence, this accumulated body of law, custom and usage stood before the Constituent Assembly as inheritance rather than destiny. The new republic asserted its authority to retain or reject it. That authority continues to reside in Parliament, so long as it acts within the bounds of constitutional competence.

Article 372 states that all laws in force within the territory of India before the Constitution came into effect shall continue until altered, repealed or amended. It is under this provision that so-called cultural rights based on custom and usage are claimed. Such arguments ignore that continuity is a matter of constitutional choice. Under the theory of discontinuity, a successor state is not compelled to preserve the legal order of its predecessor.

Read together, these two articles articulate the theory of the clean slate that we conferred upon ourselves at the commencement of the Constitution. They mark a conscious decision to found the republic on a new normative order. For that reason, arguments that we must look to an ancient past or a 5,000-year-old culture to interpret the Constitution are misplaced.

There is a legal discontinuity between ancient Indic philosophy and the modern liberal political philosophy embodied in the Constitution. The latter represents a deliberate constitutional choice, not a continuation of pre-modern forms of authority. Efforts by sections of the right to assert such continuity operate as a device to circumvent the liberal character of the Constitution without formally amending it. If the aspiration is to establish a Hindu Rashtra grounded in notions of feudal kingship, that objective cannot be reconciled with the constitutional settlement as it stands.

An attempt is being made to suggest that, as a nation, we owe allegiance to a philosophy that stands above the Constitution. Hinduism is described in judicial discourse as a 'way of life', and an effort is made to construct a seamless continuity between ancient Hindu culture and the constitutional order. From this, it is argued that when culture or religion appears to conflict with the Constitution, the former must prevail. Such reasoning is fundamentally anti-constitutional. The idea of a Hindu Rashtra is being advanced through political rhetoric, through certain judicial pronouncements, and through statutes that strain constitutional limits. At the same time, the text of the Constitution remains *largely* unamended. Its liberal and democratic character has not been formally rewritten. Fundamental rights continue to exist on paper.

Yet the lived reality tells a different story. Minorities are lynched. Journalists face prosecution or violent attack. Lawyers are targeted for discharging their professional obligations. Muslim homes are demolished, allegedly for being 'unauthorized'. Those convicted of grave crimes, including rape, are granted remission. Civil society activists are incarcerated for prolonged periods. Intellectuals are branded 'urban naxals'. Thought itself is cast as subversion, and dissent is prosecuted as an attempt at 'regime change'.

RM: Let me ask you a very direct question: Do you see progressive movement in this direction on the part of the judiciary?

IJ: Article 13 states unequivocally that any law inconsistent with fundamental rights is void. Articles 32 and 226 provide direct access to the Supreme Court and the high courts for their enforcement. Yet we find our courts choosing to virtually relinquish their power of judicial review and endorsing many decisions of the incumbent government. Since 2014, only two major Supreme Court rulings have gone decisively against the government: the judgment striking down the National Judicial Appointments Commission,[12] which preserved the court's role in judicial appointments; and the Electoral Bonds verdict[13], delivered long after vast sums of money had already been raised and spent for electoral purposes. It's almost as though the courts, acting in alignment with prevailing state policy, are permitting a cultural norm to assume primacy over the Constitution as the governing standard of public life.

The extrajudicial utterances of judges are the real giveaway. They reflect the cognitive cultural bias of judges that may or may not be apparent in judgments. Judges have grown increasingly voluble off the bench, and their extrajudicial utterances often reveal how their judicial philosophy is shaped. Speaking at the 16th National Conference of the Akhil Bharatiya Adhivakta Parishad at Kurukshetra University, Haryana, from 26–28 December 2024, Justice G.R. Swaminathan of the Madras High Court said that Article 72 of the Constitution, Section 432 of CrPC on the power of pardon, has its origins in the Valmiki Ramayana, ignoring that every sovereign democratic state holds this power! His invocation of the Valmiki Ramayana was selective, if not political; it is ahistorical to suggest a continuity of political thought between the Vedas and the Constitution.

Such attempts to link the jurisprudence of constitutional India to an ancient past illustrate a direct assault on the ethos of the Constitution, and this narrative recurs across the executive, legislature and judiciary. Justice Sharad Yadav delivered a hate speech within the premises of the high court and faced no consequences, since his hatred was directed towards Muslims. How, then, can one expect such a judge to deal with an issue such as the demolition of a Muslim household in an unbiased manner, adhering to the rule of law?

This marks the beginning of a gradual seepage of cultural norms into judicial reasoning, so that they become the reference point against which the legality of State action is assessed. It is the cognitive and cultural bias of judges that enables the abandonment of due process and the rule of law, leading to the erosion of civil and political rights. This tendency is particularly visible where cultural and religious claims come into conflict with civil and political rights.

Where interpretive latitude exists, such judges are more likely to decide with reference to cultural or religious norms rather than to civil or constitutional law. This has appeared to be a defining feature of the judiciary during periods of majoritarian government, a tendency to follow the direction in which the sun goes, what I have described as the 'surajmukhi (sunflower)' court.

This is the most insidious threat to the Constitution: the bypassing of its principles in favour of culture, here framed as Hindu culture, and presented as embodying the will or sentiments of the majority. This was starkly evident in the Ram Mandir case. The final judgment appeared to privilege faith while presenting itself as grounded in fact and law. It went further, breaching the wall of separation between religion and the State by directing the Union government to create and fund a trust to which the disputed site was to be handed over. Even if one assumes that the findings on fact were correct, it would have sufficed to decree the suit and leave the parties to pursue their remedies in accordance with ordinary legal process.

After the NJAC judgment, there was an expectation that a constitutional amendment might be introduced to recalibrate or reaffirm judicial primacy in appointments. Although, the then law minister, the late Arun Jaitley, criticized the ruling as an instance of an unelected judiciary thwarting the will of the majority. Yet, no workable amendment followed. Similar utterances have since been echoed by former law minister Kiren Rijiju and the former vice president of India, Jagdeep Dhankhar.

An independent judiciary is the most important institution of accountability. The collegium system was intended to safeguard judicial primacy in appointments, placing it over the will of the executive. While that is the principle we were led to expect, the Supreme Court's recent history tells a different story: a pattern of comfortable coexistence with the executive, marked by give-and-take in the matter of appointment of judges. Why amend the Constitution if you can do from the back door what you cannot do from the front door. Judges seen as 'difficult', or those who have ruled against any member of the ruling party, are simply not appointed, despite a collegium recommendation. Under former Chief Justice D.Y. Chandrachud's collegium (2022–24), for example, over 15 per cent of the names recommended for elevation to the high courts were not cleared by the Union, even though established procedure gives the judiciary the final say over appointments. In turn, the judiciary needs to shed its dependence on the government for judicial appointments and be transparent about whom it elevates to constitutional courts. No judge who proclaims, 'Modi is a model; he is a hero' should be appointed. When such judges resign and then contest elections on a BJP ticket, the independence of the judiciary is lost.[14] And we certainly cannot have retired chief justices accused of sexual harassment nominated to the Rajya Sabha in the name of 'serving the public'.

Another tool for shaping outcomes is the power of the 'master of the roster'. It is now widely understood that a judge's judicial philosophy determines the outcome of a case. A Chief Justice can list matters before specific judges. There is enough literature to show that successive chief justices have routed politically sensitive cases to specific judges, expecting outcomes desirable to the powers that be.[15] Although this power, ripe for manipulation, has drawn criticism, it persists.

Increasingly, courts have been reluctant to check the draconian powers of policing civil society and political opponents that the ruling party has appropriated to itself. Since 2015, there have been repeated amendments to the Prevention of Money Laundering Act (PMLA)—a criminal law—by way of money bills. Now, money bills are introduced to enact laws in relation to issues covered under Article 110 of the Constitution. They can only be introduced in the Lok Sabha. The Rajya Sabha cannot amend or reject them; it can merely make recommendations, which may or may not be accepted by the Lok Sabha. This law was upheld by the Supreme Court, which disregarded its tainted origins and left aside the question of why it was allowed to escape the scrutiny of the Rajya Sabha. One of the most shameful judgments of the Supreme Court resulted in the incarceration of the Indian civil rights activist Teesta Setalvad in June 2022. She was assisting Zakia Jafri, the widow of former Congress Party MP Ehsan Jafri, who was killed in the Gulbarg Society massacre during the 2002 Gujarat riots, where he was burnt to death. This was an attack on the very right of access to justice, let alone justice itself.

RM: What in your opinion should we be concerned about, regarding the judiciary?

IJ: I believe civil society is now the sole defender of free speech and fundamental rights. It is no wonder, then, that the government has cracked down on it through a variety of means: the use of the Enforcement Directorate, the cancellation of Foreign Contribution (Regulation) Act (FCRA) licences, tax raids, to name just a few. The judiciary has not been able to defend civil society from persecution. This, for me, is its biggest failure. Nothing in the Constitution is more precious than life and liberty, and both are today under threat, thanks to a dysfunctional or compliant judiciary.

Political opponents, human rights activists and defenders have been systematically targeted through criminal law. One of the defining strategies of the current government has been the abuse of the power of criminal law, not just in isolated cases but as a policy of governance. Prosecutorial discretion has been all but outsourced to the party in power. A new vocabulary has replaced legal language: Anyone opposed to the ruling ideology is recast as an enemy of the State, labelled an 'urban naxal' or 'anti-national' to strip them of legitimacy. In a recent court hearing in the G.N. Saibaba case,[16] which concerned the prosecution of Professor G.N. Saibaba, a former Delhi University academic convicted under the Unlawful Activities (Prevention) Act, 1967, the presiding judge remarked that 'So far as terrorist ... activities are concerned, the brain is more dangerous. Direct involvement is not necessary.'[17] Thus far, our understanding of law was that it addresses overt actions, not beliefs or ideas.

Take the use of the UAPA, and Section 124A of the IPC, the sedition provision. Both have been used against human rights defenders in the Delhi riots and Bhima Koregaon cases, for example, without a single act of violence being attributed to them. Sedition has no place in a sovereign democratic republic. Yet its definition, as it exists today, enfolds both lawful and unlawful activity. Advocacy around legitimate dissent of government policies—legal and constitutional—can still fall within the expression 'attempts to bring into hatred or contempt, or excites or attempts to excite disaffection towards the Government established by law', and be criminalized.[18] Dissent is not a crime unless accompanied by violence. Every riot resulting in violence may be a crime, yet not every riot is a UAPA crime. The Supreme Court has rightly placed sedition in abeyance; however, analogous provisions in UAPA remain, leaving activists in prison for 'unlawful activity'. As a consequence, some individuals who opposed the CAA 2019 have been accused not only of sedition, but of terrorism under UAPA in connection with the Delhi riots of February 2020, which resulted in over fifty deaths and widespread violence. The recent report of the Law Commission is shocking. It suggests retaining Section 124A in the IPC, with certain amendments to incorporate the *ratio decidendi*[19] of *Kedar Nath Singh vs State of Bihar*,[20] said to bring greater clarity to its use. Worse, the commission recommended that the jail term of three years be increased to seven. Had the Supreme Court struck down the provision, we would not have reached this point. This suggestion has now become part of the newly enacted law, all in the name of decolonization.

Similarly, those who attended the Elgar Parishad, a public meeting held in Pune, Maharashtra, in 2017 to commemorate the bicentenary of the Battle of Bhima Koregaon, later found themselves accused of sedition and terrorism under the UAPA, in what has come to be known as the Bhima Koregaon case. Provisions of the erstwhile IPC—Section 153A, on promotion of enmity between groups, and Section 298A, on outraging religious beliefs—have also been used against those protesting caste violence, on the charge of disrupting communal harmony.[21] More recently, action has been threatened even against service delivery organizations, such as Save the Children, for speaking about malnutrition, now considered by some as an anti-national activity. A new crime appears to have been invented—defaming a nation. In such cases, simply making statistical data public can now be treated as defamatory of the country! The judiciary has been unable to prevent abuse of police powers by the executive, resulting in the prolonged incarceration of accused persons with no bail. Stan Swamy, an eighty-four-year-old Jesuit priest and tribal rights activist who was arrested in the Bhima Koregaon case under the UAPA, died in judicial custody in July 2021 while awaiting the grant of bail.

Prosecution cannot be left to politicians who believe in persecution. The impunity and immunity that members of the ruling party enjoy must be undone; they must be brought to account for repeated violations of the Constitution.

RM: Are you saying that the powers that be don't need to amend or change the Constitution, that they can just bypass it?

IJ: In my view we're on the cusp of a third transformation: from ignoring the Constitution to repudiating it. For me, 28 May 2023 marked that turning point. On that day, during the inauguration of the new Parliament building, the Prime Minister ceremonially installed a Sengol—a gold-plated sceptre associated with royal authority in the Chola tradition—near the Speaker's Chair in the Lok Sabha. The government presented the Sengol as a historic symbol of the transfer of power at Independence in 1947, invoking its association with monarchical traditions in which authority is conferred through sacred ritual. Its installation was not just symbolic—it amounted, in my view, to a repudiation of republicanism. In a democracy, power flows from the people to their elected representatives. Unlike monarchies, where power is traced to divine right, in countries governed by a written Constitution, no such divine right can be claimed. Sovereignty lies with the people as a whole. The Sengol, as a symbol of divine power passed from ruler to ruler, has no business in any Parliament, old or new.

If it was indeed handed over as a symbol of the transfer of power to independent India's first prime minister—a claim that remains debated—its proper place would be Rashtrapati Bhawan, not the House of the People. Even that claim, however, has been disputed by historians, who note that the ceremony involving the Sengol was a private religious event held at Prime Minister Nehru's residence in August 1947, and was not part of the formal constitutional transfer of power.

The sight of the sceptre, before which a Prime Minister prostrates himself in Parliament, is similarly nothing less than a repudiation of secularism and of the separation between religion and the State. I believe this marks the beginning of the third transformation, where the Constitution is simply being set aside. Similarly, the consecration of the Ram Mandir in Ayodhya by Prime Minister Modi represented the complete collapse between the secular and the sacred. The Indian Constitution, seen as signifying the 'idea of India', was brushed aside.[22] During his address at the Pran Pratishtha ceremony of the Ram Temple in Ayodhya on 22 January 2024, the prime minister is reported to have said explicitly, 'Ram is the idea of India.'[23] This implied that a return to Ram Rajya would be the true decolonization of India.

Much has been written about the 1975 Emergency. It is true that fundamental rights were suspended then, but what we have witnessed over the past decade is of a different order: the suspension of the Constitution itself, followed by its repudiation. This has been enabled through a climate of impunity brought on primarily by the judiciary looking askance when governmental action or inaction has been challenged. Whether it was demonetization, the challenge to the CAA, or the abrogation of Article 370, the judiciary stood aside. When notice is not issued on a petition under Article 32 (the right to constitutional remedies), which guarantees the right to seek constitutional remedies for violations of fundamental rights, the Constitution's protective mechanism is not merely deferred, it is effectively put in cold storage or suspended. The discretion lies with the judiciary.

In the present era, constitutional law is being defeated by statutory laws, and by the abuse of law raised to the level of policy. Statutes such as the Prevention of Money Laundering Act, 2002, or UAPA are invoked in cases where they have no application. The courts have acknowledged as much, time and again, but are reluctant to strike down these draconian powers.

RM: Are you suggesting that the judiciary is unable to protect the right to dissent?

IJ: I am saying the judiciary is unable to defend the Constitution. I am not the one dissenting; I am affirming the Constitution of India when I speak up. It is the party in power, the Government of India, that is repudiating the Constitution each time I exercise my right to invoke it in my defence. All governments fear a Constitution as they would prefer to function without one. It seems the courts are adding invisible ink to the Constitution—interpretations that can turn it on its head, from protecting our lives and rights to imposing duties we owe to the State.

When the abuse of law becomes policy, it begins to pass for the new normal and few dare to challenge it. Fear and bribery combine to prevent citizens from exercising their rights. Mahatma Gandhi, writing in *Young India*, on 29 January 1925, said:

> Real Swaraj will come not by acquisition of authority by a few, but by the acquisition of the capacity by all to resist authority when it is abused. In other words, Swaraj is to be obtained by educating the masses to a sense of their capacity to regulate and control authority.

It is this swaraj that we need to appropriate. This is what azadi means to us. Lawyers should be guardians of law and liberty and, as such, are interested in keeping the statute book of the country 'pure and undefiled'.[24] Today, it is also our duty to ensure that the Constitution does not become a museum piece, consigned to the dustbin of history.

8

DOING JUSTICE

RM: On the question of accountability, I recall your intervention some years ago when allegations of corruption were made against a sitting judge of the court …

IJ: Let me begin with what I mean by 'doing justice'. I believe we have a right to get justice in real time. This means we are the first line of defence of our own rights. Any violation of your rights must first and foremost be defended by us as a matter of self-defence. We must resist injustice where we see it, in real time. When I see injustice on my own doorstep, I speak up. That, for me, is doing justice. Democracy and accountability begin at your doorstep. This is how my interest in the accountability of the judiciary started. It was on a flight from Bombay to Delhi in December 1989, when I was due to appear in one of the cases relating to the Bhopal Gas Tragedy, that I read a short column in *Mid-Day*, tucked away in an inconspicuous corner. It reported that a sitting judge of the Supreme Court had been accused of corruption for expenses he had incurred while serving as Chief

Justice of the Punjab and Haryana High Court. The details were shocking: bedsheets and pillow covers for his daughter's dowry, carpets and other items far exceeding the sanctioned entitlements for judges and so on. I remember thinking: Is this the court I am going to migrate to from Bombay?

Fortunately, the report had a byline: Kuldip Nayar. Once in Delhi, I was determined to meet him and get the details. I called him, and he said, 'I will get back to you.' Perhaps it was to verify my intent. A few days later, he asked me to meet him at the India International Centre in Delhi, where he told me that every word of the report could be substantiated by internal documents. He pointed me to people who could help locate those documents, and I did. Together with the legal luminary K.G. Kannabiran and my colleague K. Chandru, who later became a judge of the Madras High Court, we co-authored an article for *The Lawyers*. The cover story, titled 'Judicial Corruption', carried a photograph of Justice V. Ramaswami, the accused judge. It was the first time the word 'corruption' had been used in print in connection with a sitting Supreme Court judge. We published the full text of the internal audit report, containing the details of his financial misconduct.[1]

People would often say, 'We know magistrates are corrupt, but not Supreme Court judges.' Our story blew this myth open. Justice Ramaswami was eventually impeached, but the motion for his removal in Parliament failed when the Congress party abstained from voting on it. Even so, the then CJI, the late Sabyasachi Mukherjee—a judge of great sensitivity—asked him to go on leave. He never returned to the bench and retired in 1992.

It would be apposite to quote from the statement made by Justice Mukherjee made to the bar regarding the conduct of Justice V. Ramaswami:

> The Supreme Court must uphold the rule of law. It is, therefore, necessary that those who uphold the rule of law live by law and judges must, therefore, be obliged to live according to law. The law, procedure and the norms applicable in this case, enjoin that the expenses incurred by the Court for the Judges must be according to the rules, norms and the practice. No man is above law or the rules. The Judges either of the Supreme Court or of the High Courts and the Chief Justices are all subject to the rule of law and procedure like any other citizen of this country and must abide by the norms and regulation prescribed inasmuch as these and to the extent are applicable to them.[2]

Judicial behaviour today has become increasingly secretive and non-transparent, unlike the openness once shown by Chief Justice Mukherjee. Since then, I have had an abiding interest in the question of judicial accountability. To the extent possible, I have focused my attention on judicial appointments and on improving the infrastructure of justice in ways that promote gender sensitivity and bringing feminist perspectives into the courts. From protesting the sexual harassment of women judicial officers to demanding a crèche in the Supreme Court; from pushing for transparency in the designation of senior advocates to advocating for more women in senior positions—these have been my concerns. But times have changed. When I approached Chief Justice Mukherjee in 1990 with a complaint against Justice

Ramaswami, there was genuine engagement with the issue. Today, we are met with silence when we approach the CJI with a complaint, such as in the case of Justice Shekhar Kumar Yadav of the Allahabad High Court, against whom a formal complaint was submitted following his public remarks that reflected clear political and religious bias.[3]

Someone recently asked me why I care so deeply about the way lawyers are designated as seniors. My answer came instinctively. Democracy begins at your place of work. Of course, it begins at home too, and it begins in the kitchen, as you know, but it also begins where you labour and build your life. For me, that place has always been the Supreme Court of India and the high courts. Ever since I joined the bar, and perhaps this comes from being a woman, I noticed certain patterns of hegemony in the legal profession and the judiciary. Dynasty within the profession was one of the most obvious. Sons of lawyers were lawyers, and this meant sons of judges were judges. Caste and class determined whether you would be designated a senior or become a judge. The seniors you see around you are not necessarily defined by experience or merit. You notice that it is the sons of judges who are designated as seniors. You see how privilege is selective, how the profession has become a monopoly of the few. So when people ask why I chose to challenge the system, I say it was an idea whose time had come. I was already a designated senior and hence could not be accused of going to court to seek justice for myself. The inequities were always visible; I simply decided to challenge them.

That happened in 2015, when I filed a petition in court questioning the arbitrariness of the system. I asked: Could the court be so inconsistent and unaccountable in the way it chose lawyers for designation as seniors, such that only sons of judges and former seniors were designated? I insisted that there had to be clear guidelines, not necessarily based on merit, but certainly on performance. Even performance, as I pointed out, depends on opportunity. You can only prove your ability if you are given the chance to do so. There is no getting away from the fact that opportunity, in turn, is linked to privilege.

From my own experience, I realized that I lacked a certain privilege that seemed to define advancement in the legal profession. I did not belong to a family of lawyers or to a community that could open doors for me. I had not migrated with a job waiting for me, and I was not an MP or a law officer. What I did have was passion for my work. When I was eventually designated a senior, I saw it as recognition of my passion and professionalism, not privilege. And I thought, if I could do it, others should be able to as well. That conviction is what drove me to challenge the court. I said then, and I still believe, that the judiciary must be transparent in its functioning.

In 2017, we received a judgment holding that objective criteria must govern the designation of seniors. It was a major breakthrough for the structure of the legal profession, which, in my view, had long been losing its sense of professionalism. Frankly, it had become a failing profession. Leave aside passion, even legal talent has become scarce as the profession has increasingly turned into a money-making enterprise. I was very pleased with that judgment. But, as with so many efforts to democratize our institutions, it faced resistance. Before the ink was even dry, the judgment was challenged. An argument made was that recognizing talent was the court's prerogative; designation was an honour, and honours could not be demanded or applied for. The 2017 ruling was eventually reversed, and power was returned to the court to exercise its discretion.

At the time of writing, a review petition filed by me is pending, awaiting a hearing. The battle for equal justice will go on. The shift it set in motion is irreversible, for it has awakened aspirations among a class of lawyers with no godfathers or godmothers, but determined to advance on the strength of their performance.

Let's come to the question of a crèche. There had never been one in the Supreme Court of India. I had a junior who would bring her little daughter to court every day; the child sat outside on the lawn with her maid, under the shade of a tree. One day I told her, 'This is not acceptable. I can't have you working for me in these conditions. Let's go to court and demand a crèche.' So we did.

Today, the Supreme Court has a beautiful, state-of-the-art crèche. Every detail was carefully planned, including the kind of food that children could bring. We insisted that no junk food or any artificial drinks be allowed. This facility has enabled women to come to court without a sense of guilt at leaving their children at home. Members of the court staff have been among its greatest beneficiaries. It is heartwarming to see fathers bring their children to the crèche when their wives are at work in the corporate sector, breaking gender stereotypes.

The third issue, closely linked to the others, was a petition I filed seeking live-streaming of Supreme Court proceedings. This was another attempt to promote accountability. At the time, there were countless cases with no official record of what had been argued in court. Too often, judgments attributed statements to lawyers that had never been made. The real solution was either to produce full transcripts of proceedings or live-stream them. Once again, I went to court over the issue. The petition succeeded.

Sometimes I do ask myself: why me? Why didn't anybody else file these petitions? There are so many women working in the Supreme Court. But there is always a trigger, always a moment that compels action. Ultimately, I just want to say that there is a case for feminizing the infrastructure of the court, for reimagining the spaces and systems through which justice is delivered. Doing justice, for me, means resisting in real time.

There have been times when male judges and lawyers have made sexist remarks against me in open court. I have pointed this out immediately and demanded that they stop. The culture of sycophancy has not prevented me from calling out judges or lawyers as they speak, rather than filing cases against them in the future. When a senior colleague refers to you as someone's wife, it is time to stop them in their tracks. When a judge, yielding to the influence of senior male colleagues appearing against you, says, 'We have had the pleasure of hearing you. Dismissed,' it is time to tell them in open court that we go there for work, not for their pleasure.

Help yourself to justice before expecting someone else to help you. Tell your colleagues and the judges when they are behaving like male chauvinists, and they will change. Refuse to be subservient in your daily interactions with them.

9

THE RULE OF LAW

RM: We've had a wide-ranging discussion. Now I'd like to pose a final question to you, on the very notion of justice and what it entails.

IJ: Implicit in our conversations is the question: what is justice? To begin with, justice is a demand on the State. Every time I enter a courtroom, I ask myself why I am there, and the answer is always: 'to look for justice'. The Preamble promises justice—social, economic and political. Each client who has come to me has said, 'I want justice.' When I ask them, 'What does justice mean to you?', their replies remind me that justice means something different, something unique, to each person. It is shaped by their needs, the stage of life they are in, and perhaps by their philosophy of life or material situation.

My clients have often asked me simple questions:

Is it fair that my husband throws me out of my house empty-handed?

Is it fair that I cannot hawk to earn a living?

Is it fair that, as a homeless person, I am evicted without an alternative to live and work?

Is it fair that I get kicked around by a policeman, or that I am imprisoned without trial until I am close to dying?

Is it fair that I am raped by my husband or subjected to violence from my intimate partner?

Is it fair that I cannot marry a person of my choice?

Is it fair that coming from historic disadvantage, I am asked to compete with a person of privilege on their terms? Is that what equality of opportunity means?

Justice requires that the law provides answers to these questions, grounded in a value system that is not negotiable.

This inevitably raises another question: What is fairness? In our civilizational ethos and contemporary understanding, fairness means that society's resources must be distributed to serve the common good. This is what our Constitution mandates and why it remains a modern Constitution.

The notion of social and economic justice is relatively clear. It is articulated in the Directive Principles of State Policy, and most claims to such justice can be resolved with reference to these principles.

What political justice means—beyond the right to vote and proportionate representation in elected bodies—remains less clearly defined and may be the subject of future litigation.

What has created confusion in our minds is the definition of criminal justice. The Constitution guarantees that no person will be deprived of life and liberty except by due process of law, the right against self-incrimination, protection against double jeopardy and the all-important right against retrospective criminality. The IPC and the CrPC, now replaced by the Bharatiya

Nyaya Sanhita (BNS) and Bharatiya Nagarik Suraksha Sanhita (BNSS), guarantee due process in criminal prosecution by the State. Crime is what a society holds to be morally reprehensible. Although crime is defined in the code with clarity, punishment itself is not defined, vesting large discretion in judges to determine sentencing. What is worse, there is no clarity on what must guide this discretion in matters of punishment, or what the object and purpose of punishment should be. Is it to seek revenge for the victim? Is it to deter others from committing crime? Is it to seek vindication for wrongdoing? Or is it to reform the accused?

RM: Could you just historicize the concept of justice?

IJ: The evolution of intellectual thought on what constitutes justice has taken distinct forms across various historical periods and regions. It goes back more than 4,000 years. The codification of law played a major role in setting out people's expectations of their rulers and monarchs. Written laws gave citizens the means to claim equality of treatment in all disputes, whether civil or criminal.

The civil domain covered trade, commerce, contracts and property, while crime referred to acts the ruler deemed wrongful. These were offences that could invite corporal punishment or the denial of life and liberty. Each society decided for itself what constituted proportionate punishment, depending on the gravity of the crime, though most accepted the death penalty for what they considered heinous crimes. All rulers, in their own way, promised a better life to those they governed.

Long before the ideas of 'constitutionalism' and 'citizenship' emerged as categories of governance and rights, rulers invoked the promise of 'justice' to legitimize their authority. Law was a means of maintaining order, and every society linked to it a vision of an ideal cosmic order. The rulers claimed to ensure 'justice' among their subjects by adjudicating private disputes. There was, however, no question of the monarch himself being governed by the rule of law; he was the lawgiver.

Across history, spanning centuries and continents, jurists and scholars have helped rulers define what justice meant. The great ancient civilizations each developed their own conception of justice, depending on their understanding of cosmic order. In Mesopotamia, rulers wrote down codes that dealt with both civil disputes and crimes. These codes were created not for the rulers, but the ruled. Their function was to set standards that ordinary people could invoke against those who sought to oppress them, whether through bodily deprivation or the seizure of property. From this impulse emerged the Code of Hammurabi,[1] in which criminal justice rested on the doctrines of revenge and retribution. To legitimize their rule, Mesopotamian rulers also promised social and economic justice, linking order with moral and material well-being.

In India, the Hindus had developed a highly codified system of law known as the Dharmashastras, with Brahmins playing a key role both in governance and in dispensing justice according to them. They held the exclusive authority to anoint kings and to declare them rulers of the land. They also performed the rituals and sacrifices prescribed in the Vedas to sanctify royal power. The king, in turn, was believed to possess the divine right to rule and to secure justice for their people. But this process was mediated by the Brahmins and religious scholars who interpreted the shastras.

It is important to remember, however, that the Dharmashastras were based not on the rights of the people, but on the duties of both the king and the governed. Justice meant fidelity to dharma, the moral and social order laid down in the scriptures. The ruler embodied dharma and, therefore, of justice itself. It is from this conception that the ideal of Ram Rajya arose as a vision of perfect governance.

When the Prime Minister declared that 'Ram is the idea of India', he was invoking an ancient conception of rule that ignores centuries of evolution in law and constitutionalism, i.e., the principle that those who govern are as much subject to the law as those whom they govern. Under the caste system entrenched in the Dharmashastras, dharma meant carrying out duties expected of one's caste. It covered every aspect of life: the duty of marriage and procreation; the religious duties of a householder; duties of men, women and children; and rules of property and inheritance. Justice was defined by one's caste duty, and punishment depended on caste status: A Brahmin could not be found guilty of a crime, not even murder. From time immemorial, India has never drawn a clear line between religion and law. Many of our modern-day problems remain bedevilled by this legacy.

RM: You mentioned three major civilizations ...

IJ: Yes. The Chinese emperors had a very different approach to law and justice. For them, order meant discipline, punishment and reward, not social justice. Unlike the Hindus, they did not have Brahmins telling them what to do. The law was an instrument of political power, rather than justice. The system lasted for centuries, until Confucius argued that social stability depended on the relationship between ruler and ruled. Yet at no point was the ruler himself governed by the rule of law.

The contrast between the Mesopotamian, Hindu and Chinese systems is striking. As one author observed, both Mesopotamian and Hindus kings codified laws but 'while the Mesopotamian kings were mapping social justice, the brahmins were specifying individual duties with cosmological order in mind'.[2]

There were three cultures in which law was never separated from religion: Jewish, Hindu and Islamic. In each, religion governed every aspect of life, from birth to death, and even before and after. But for me, justice has always meant the separation of religion from law.

The notion of enforceable rights, as we know them today, emerged in the Western world in the seventeenth century. In the United Kingdom, for instance, the shift away from justice as divine dispensation—delivered by kings—the separation of church and state also entailed the sovereignty of the people in governing themselves. The conception of rights 'inherent' to being human came from this. While there are different ways of understanding rights, whether as natural, inherent or those created by law, there is agreement on one issue: Our societies are governed by the rule of law. This means that rights are available to citizens against governments bound by the same laws as the citizens. Constitutionalism, as we understand it today, is based on the idea that a written document binds both ruler and ruled, and that rights can be enforced against the State by an independent judiciary. Government functions by consent, wherein the sovereignty lies with the people. Parliamentary sovereignty of law-making is subject to judicial review: Laws may be declared unconstitutional and struck down. We still live with the legal fiction of 'social contract', whereby we agree, via contract, to be governed by our elected representatives while retaining the right to change them through periodic elections.

RM: All this would have been quite antithetical to notions of dharma …

IJ: India's journey to the rule of law was inspired by not only global developments in constitutionalism, but also its own anti-colonial struggle. To understand this journey, we must first ask what colonization meant for the rule of law in India. One of the central keys to justifying foreign rule was the codification of criminal laws. So, we were given the three criminal codes, making us heirs to the legacy of the Magna Carta: the idea that no person can be deprived of life and liberty without due process of law, and that justice is not a divine function but a function of governance. This laid the foundation for a professional judiciary independent of the executive and a class of lawyers who defended people in open court. The law, in principle, applied equally to all, without distinction of caste, class, gender or religion. Commercial and property laws were also codified, drawing on the law of merchants and the rules of private ownership, respectively.

However, the Constitution of India does not spell out an overt theory of justice, even though its Preamble promises social, economic and political justices. Implicit in any of its conceptions is the question of values and meaning, i.e., a vision of the good life that must be quarantined from those who govern. The redistribution of resources is written into the Directive Principles of State Policy, which guarantee social and economic justice. Political justice is guaranteed by adult franchise, with each person counting as one. Fundamental rights are also guaranteed: the right to life and liberty; the right to hold opinions; freedom of conscience; the right to free speech and expression (subject to limitations of public order, defamation and morality); the right to move freely throughout the territory of India; to associate freely; and to practise one's religion.

For me, this amounts to a theory of justice. It is a justice that allows each person to live the way they choose, limited only by the equal right of others to do the same and by what is called the 'harm principle'. The autonomy of being is guaranteed, subject only to the autonomy of the others in equal measure.

Justice, in this sense, comprises the aspirations of all humans: that equality of opportunity, treatment and outcome is due to us all. For me, the function of both justice and law is to enable life as we know it on earth to flourish in all its dimensions. This morality and ethic must govern the making of laws and their implementation by the courts.

RM: We live in a multilingual, multifaith, multiethnic society, with diverse customs and practices ...

IJ: A theory of justice cannot concern itself with what came before birth or after death. Its subject is earthly justice: the human body and the society we inhabit. The domain of law, then, is sentient human beings, both as individuals and as members of a society. God may or may not exist, but revelation is hearsay, not evidence, and lies outside the ambit of law. The existence of a god is a belief, a concept, an idea. Beliefs differ, as do notions of god. To enforce one belief on all cannot be reconciled with ideals of liberty, equality, fraternity, dignity and complete justice as promised in our Constitution's Preamble.

Belief in a singular god, in a multifaith world, can have no place in any evolving society. It threatens the species with extinction and undermines the unity of any nation, forming the basis of our secularism. When a multifaith society like India moves towards theocracy—by, say, enacting laws against blasphemy—it invites disunity, internal attacks and external aggression.

No theory of justice requires the concept of a god, howsoever conceived, to bring order, meaning or purpose to the universe or to human life.

During the colonial period, criminal law was both secular and equal across religions. In that sense, religion and law were completely delinked in the criminal realm; civil law was not. Hindus were governed by Hindu law—later known as the Anglo-Hindu law, based on the Dharmashastras as interpreted by British judges—and Muslims by the Sharia. As a consequence, judges today, appointed under a secular Constitution, are still required to interpret religious texts. And even after Hindu law was codified post-Independence, its origins in dharma are often retained, leaving judges to interpret and rely on religious precept when statutes are ambiguous.

For me, the unfinished agenda of the Indian Constitution, and of justice itself, is the full separation of religion and law. Yet in our courts we continue to swear in the name of God, as if truth depends on the threat of 'hell'.

RM: Let's take up the question of fundamental rights.

IJ: Central to the conferment of rights is the human body as the repository of rights. Gandhi understood that the injustice of the State becomes visible when the body is subjected to violence.

Of all rights, the most important is the right to life and liberty, i.e., the right not to be deprived of it. There are many ways in which the right to life is violated, but the most obvious of them is the death penalty. I would argue that the death penalty should be abolished. Civilization gave up retribution as the goal of justice long ago, focusing instead on circumstances that engender crime and on prevention rather than punishment. Compassion must be central to any notion or dispensation of justice. The role of a judge in the modern world is not to mete out sanctions but to understand the circumstances and context in which crimes are committed, and to prevent their recurrence. By no means has the death penalty proved effective in preventing crime; it is, therefore, barbaric. Prisons, too, across the world, have failed to provide conditions compatible with life, making incarceration itself a suspect form of punishment, until such conditions are created.

It may be normal for victims to seek retribution, but not for a judge. The distance between judge and victim must be scrupulously maintained. If judges equate justice with revenge, they would be no different from a criminal.

Justice is contextual. It is a promise of non-repetition, an assurance of the veracity of systems, of society and of collective conscience in pursuit of the common good. Every protest that shakes the foundations of power demands not just accountability but an assurance that such atrocities will never recur. Justice cannot be confined to a courtroom or reduced to a penal code; it must be expansive, inclusive and forward-looking. Protests serve as catalysts for justice. They awaken systems from their slumber and force them to act. The demand for justice does not arise in a vacuum; it is forged in the crucible of collective dissent.

In its truest sense, justice must mean more. Thabo Mbeki, the President of South Africa from 1999 to 2008, illustrated this during his role as chief mediator of the African Union High-Level Implementation Panel on Sudan, which was tasked with addressing the Darfur conflict—a brutal civil war marked by mass killings, displacement and allegations of genocide. During meetings with Sudanese communities affected by the violence, many expressed anguish over why Omar al-Bashir, Sudan's then President, who had been indicted by the International Criminal Court for genocide, crimes against humanity and war crimes, had not been arrested. Mbeki challenged them to define justice for themselves. What, he asked, was their ultimate goal? Was it peace, reconciliation, democracy and justice? Or simply seeing al-Bashir behind bars? And could justice entail restitution, compensation or apologies?

These were not abstract questions. His inquiry reveals a profound truth: Justice must be rooted in the lived experiences and aspirations of those who seek it. It must promise more than punishment; it must promise change.

In India, this broader vision of justice often seems elusive. The outrage ignited by the horrific violence in Kathua in 2018, where an eight-year-old girl from a nomadic Muslim community was abducted, raped and murdered; in Hathras in 2020, where a young Dalit woman died after being brutally assaulted, and her body was cremated by the authorities without her family's consent; and in Manipur in 2023, where women from the Kuki-Zo tribal community were subjected to sexual violence amid ethnic conflict, exposes the systemic and structural failures that enable such violence. Rape, as an atrocity, is rarely a standalone act. It is a manifestation of caste, communal and patriarchal oppressions embedded in the fabric of society. Unless we confront these interwoven injustices, justice will remain partial and its promise unfulfilled. Protests remind us of what is possible. Time and again, they have shown that even the mightiest governments can be held to account.

Yet justice demands more than episodic victories. It requires systemic reform and a commitment to non-repetition. It must ensure accountability and dismantle the conditions that allow atrocities to occur. It is not enough to punish the offender or enact laws in response to public outcry. We must ask, as Mbeki did: What is our ultimate goal? Is it merely to punish the guilty, or to build a society where such guilt never arises? Justice, then, is not a destination but a journey—a continuous effort to transform outrage into action, suffering into solidarity and violence into peace.

RM: I'd like you to talk about what this has meant for you, in practice, in court.

IJ: Every case I have argued has brought me back to the same question. Let me begin with the death penalty: Do the means justify the end? These are as much ethical as moral questions. If we truly wish to change the society we live in, we must look at the conditions in which crimes occur, rather than seeking to erase the criminal from existence.

Around the time those convicted of Nirbhaya's rape and murder were about to be executed in March 2020—following their conviction for the gang rape and murder of a young woman in Delhi in December 2012, a horrific crime that sparked nationwide protests and led to significant reforms in India's criminal law—I tweeted an appeal to her parents to forgive the condemned. I cited Sonia Gandhi's example. She forgave Nalini Sriharan, who had been convicted for her role in the assassination of former Prime Minister Rajiv Gandhi in 1991, and did not press for the death penalty. Nalini's death sentence was commuted to life imprisonment in 2000 after Sonia Gandhi expressed her opposition to her execution in a clemency petition addressed to the Tamil Nadu governor. More than two decades later, in November 2022, the Supreme Court ordered Nalini's release, along with other convicts in the case, after she had spent over thirty years in prison. After her release, she expressed a wish to reunite with her daughter, who lives in the United Kingdom.

For my tweet, I was trolled on social media, most notably on X (then Twitter). Among those who responded was actor and member of Parliament Kangana Ranaut, who said about me, in response to a question by a journalist, 'That lady should be kept in jail with those convicts for four days.[3]' What was she expressing here? Pure hatred. How was she any different from the criminals who were to be hanged? Hatred affects, first and foremost, the person who hates; it is the fruit of a poisoned tree. The principles of criminal justice must be articulated in a manner that allows for recantation and the reintegration of the guilty into society.

Often, the remedy lies in acknowledging the injustice done to the victim by the predator, paired with a genuine expression of remorse by the convicted and a guarantee that such acts will not be repeated. One incident that immediately comes to mind is the case of those convicted in the Bilkis Bano case, which arose out of the communal violence that followed the 2002 Gujarat riots. Bilkis Bano, then five months pregnant, was gangraped, and fourteen members of her family, including her young child, were murdered while they were fleeing the violence. In 2008, a special CBI court convicted eleven men for gang rape and murder and sentenced them to life imprisonment. However, in August 2022, the state of Gujarat granted remission to all eleven convicts and released them after they had served over fourteen years in prison. Following their release, several of them publicly denied having committed the crimes. Their denial was shocking enough, but worse still was the way they were received back into society—as heroes of the riots, celebrated for supposedly defending Hindu 'honour'.

In 2022, I represented MP Mahua Moitra in a petition challenging the remission granted to the convicts, arguing that the remission was bad in law: they had falsely claimed to have spent fourteen years in custody (the minimum period for eligibility), and they had been convicted of rape and murder during a genocide-like situation. While I do not oppose remission as a general principle, it was necessary to point out that under international criminal law, sentences for crimes such as genocide may extend to thirty years or life imprisonment, depending on the gravity of the offence and the circumstances of the accused. International law, notably, does not provide for the death penalty even for genocide.

I recall another case involving a woman whose husband was shot dead in cold blood by her own parents, who had hired a contract killer. Her parents and brother were charged as co-conspirators along with the shooter. The brother was acquitted, as he was not present at the scene of the crime. To her, this did not feel like justice. Her parents and the shooter were convicted, but when her mother surrendered in court, she turned to her son and said, 'You have been acquitted. We too will soon be out.' The daughter, who had hoped at last to taste victory, collapsed when she saw that her mother felt no remorse. Her mother rejoiced in her son's acquittal; her daughter's life meant nothing to her. In her eyes, the true crime was her daughter's act of crossing caste boundaries by marrying outside her caste. Where, then, was justice for the daughter, even though her parents had been sentenced to life? None, she felt. A conviction offered no comfort when there was no remorse. She now faced the renewed fear of another attack and remained an outcast from her family. Justice was still out of reach. She told me that justice, for her, would have meant the village acknowledging the crimes of her parents.

It is therefore heartening that in January 2024, a bench led by Justice B.V. Nagarathna, alongside Justice Ujjal Bhuyan, set aside the remission granted to the convicts in *Bilkis Yakub Rasool vs Union of India*—one of the rare success stories of the Supreme Court.

RM: Assassination and murder are extreme cases. But you must have dealt with others that were less grave?

IJ: Oh, yes. The hawkers of Bombay asked me: If merchants and businessmen have the right to trade, why don't we? The pavement dwellers asked: If you have the right to live in your homes, why can't we build one for ourselves? Why does the law not leave us alone? Are we just 'benches and boxes' to be picked up and thrown out of the city?

The Air India air hostesses asked: If men can be supervisors, why can't we? If women can be pilots, why can't air hostesses oversee the passenger cabin?

Women cast out of their matrimonial homes asked: Do we not have a share in our own homes? Women facing sexual harassment asked: Why are there no women on the bench to hear our cases?

Dalits asked me: Why are we still underrepresented in higher public service? Dalit lawyers asked: Why are we not being made judges? Many women asked: Why do our husbands still have the right to rape us?

Githa Hariharan asked: I give birth to my child and raise it. Why is the father the 'natural guardian'? Mary Roy asked: Why am I entitled to only ₹5,000 from my father's estate while my brother inherits the rest?

If the function of law is to preserve order and advance the public good, each of these people was entitled to an answer from the court. When I think of the case I argued for the hawkers of Bombay, the image that comes to mind is of a woman selling bananas in a basket at a busy street intersection. A policeman walks up to her, orders her to leave, kicks the basket, crushes the bananas under his boots and walks away. How different is he from the then chief minister of Maharashtra, A.R. Antulay, who, during the full fury of the Bombay monsoon, ordered thousands of pavement dwellers to be crammed into buses and dumped outside the state without offering them alternate shelter?

In each of these cases the pavement dwellers and hawkers, were living orderly lives, serving an equally orderly community through their labour and the provision of services. This fragile order required only to be left alone or gently regulated, not destroyed. On the pavements, I saw life in its fullest form—women cooking, cleaning and drying clothes; children being born, people dying; funerals being held—and, all the while, pavement dwellers providing services to their fellow citizens.

Where others saw 'squalor' and 'nuisance', I saw life in motion and struggle.

When I argued the hawkers' case in the Supreme Court, a judge snapped and said, 'Ms Jaising, do you realize that they are only licencees, not owners, of the premises?' I answered, 'Do you realize that this very building in which you sit is on licence to the Supreme Court of India, or that the electricity that is supplied to you and the water in your taps is on licence to you too?' He was stunned, then reprimanded me for daring to question a judge's knowledge of law.

The moment passed with me in tears. Then came the rebuke: that I should be 'more like Mr Grover, who is calm in court'. Adding insult to injury was casual male chauvinism.

RM: How then should justice be conceptualized?

IJ: Life as we know it—our lived experiences—are integral to any theory of justice and, therefore, of governance. I see the universe as an ordered system of relationships between all beings, sentient and non-sentient alike. It rests on interconnectedness within the universe and among humans, bound by trust and respect for individual autonomy and well-being. Buddhists seek to address the cause of suffering; so, too, must the law: to end suffering in all its forms. The State is an external agent, with a monopoly on force, regulating social relations. But what social relations does it seek to protect? They are our shared desire for peace and non-violence, without which the pursuit of happiness is impossible.

Yet the system of governance we have chosen grants the State an absolute monopoly over violence in the name of maintaining public order. Our individual demands for autonomy and self-respect encounter the equal demand of others. This mutual exchange takes place on the basis of trust and the human need for community, peace and fraternity. Unlike all other sentient beings, we have the capacity to change the quality of our lives. It obliges us to conceive the change we wish to see.

As a citizen of India, I expect my laws to address life—not pre-life, not the afterlife. I expect my right to live to be protected and respected. My life is defined by my body, so I also expect the right to bodily integrity. My body may not be invaded or assaulted; the law must protect me from such harm. Physical injury of any kind causes pain, and our instinct for survival tells us to avoid pain in order to live. It is impossible to measure the extent of trauma caused by corporal punishment, or to declare that a certain degree is bearable and thus permissible. The trauma of an assault can last a lifetime. With every lynching, every arrest, every raid, every ban and punitive action, tyranny prevails. These cruelties have been, and continue to be, inflicted on people. What is the law going to do about them?

I also expect the law to protect all citizens, irrespective of age, gender, social status or religion as it is only together that we constitute a nation. A nation is defined by its people, and people are defined by their bodies, the irrefutable proof of their existence. All human beings share similar bodies and similar requirements for nurture and sustenance. The purpose of all laws is to enable human life to flourish. Justice must focus on the primary needs of the human body as we know it. A friend of mine once put it well: If asked the question, 'What property do you own?' the only answer can be, 'My body is my only property.' No one can take it from me while I am alive.

Each morning in court, I raise my eyes above the judges on the dais to the inscription above them: 'Yato Dharamastato

Jayah (Where there is dharma, there is victory)'. It was Justice Kurian Joseph, a retired judge of the Supreme Court, who said publicly in 2024 that this motto must change to become religion-neutral. The concept of dharma belongs to an earlier era of kingship, when rulers were expected to govern in accordance with divine revelation. This idea must evolve to keep in tune with constitutionalism, under which all power is circumscribed by the Constitution, everyone is accountable to the law and an independent judiciary exists to uphold justice in citizens' interaction with the State. Perhaps the inscription should instead affirm that this is the space where you can seek justice: social, economic, political.

Be that as it may, the judges themselves are unable to see this. Once, when a bench failed to grasp the justice of an argument, I said to them, 'Your tragedy is that you enter the court from the back door so you cannot see what is written above your heads; my advantage is that I enter the court from the front and it is the first thing I see.'

Today we are told that our culture predates our Constitution, and that it is culture to which we must turn to determine our identity and interpret our laws. We are told that the Constitution is 'colonial', that duties should replace rights, culture must stand in for constitutionalism.

But what is culture? True culture is an environment that promotes growth. The purpose of law, too, is to enable life to flourish. That's why I expect the law to permit each of us to grow and flourish.

RM: You have spoken about your three migrations: from Karachi to Bombay after the Partition; from Bombay to Delhi, when you began practising in the Supreme Court; and a third, which you describe as 'home to myself'. Does this mean you are thinking of retiring?

IJ: There was a time when I thought that the word 'retirement' made sense. I mean the word itself, not mine or yours. But I now realize I was linking it to linear time. I have since come to believe there is no such thing as linear time, certainly not in my life. On the contrary, it feels more like coming full circle. From my experience, I have found that oppression and resistance go hand in hand; one cannot exist without the other. That understanding has been the driving force of my life.

At every step, I have faced some form of oppression. You may call it oppression, repression, a setback, discrimination or simply the absence of diversity. Whatever name you give it, each instance has provoked from me an instinctive pushback, which has shaped the cases I have taken on, the work I have done in court and the choices I have made in my personal life. It is this realization that makes the idea of retirement seem meaningless to me now. When I say that my third migration is 'home to myself', I mean I am completing a circle. In that sense, it is a migration, but not a retirement, for the cycle will begin again.

RM: I was struck by this formulation, because you've said repeatedly, and with conviction, that the Constitution is your home. So when you said that you were 'coming home to myself'—a very poetic, very evocative way of putting it—home seemed to be a recurring motif ...

IJ: As far as I am concerned, home is resistance.

ACKNOWLEDGEMENTS

Once again, where do I begin and where do I end?

Perhaps I must begin, as one does, with my parents. In 2005, when I was awarded the Padma Shri—one of the country's civilian honours—by the Government of India, the first person I spoke to was my father, Bansilal Jaising. I told him I wished to bring the citation home for him to see. When he read it, he did not seem surprised. His matter-of-fact words, 'You will go further,' have stayed with me. I left the citation in my parents' home, where it remained, beautifully framed, until his passing.

My mother, Vidya, responded in her usual way. She just asked, 'How are you?' She had been named by her own father, who believed, as in the Hindu tradition, that the greatest daan of all is vidya daan, i.e., the gift of knowledge. Despite being denied formal education, she educated herself through her love of books. In different ways, both my parents shaped who I became, and I remain deeply grateful to them.

My two brothers, Prakash and Vinod, who, despite our many ideological differences, have, along with their families, supported me all my life.

Anand, my life partner, who set me free to be the person I am today. Every now and then, when we are at a social event, he is approached by individuals who ask him, 'How do you live with such a strong woman?' This question reflects the deep-rooted male chauvinism that surrounds us. Yet never has he been affected by it or felt threatened and remains, to this day—over fifty years of partnership—his own person.

Ritu Menon, whom I have known for over forty years as a friend, a feminist author and publisher, for the time she spent with me and for the way she guided me to look within myself and reflect on my motivations for being the person I am. Monologues are boring, but conversations can stimulate. This book, in many ways, ended up being a conversation between two friends, each on a journey towards justice in our own way. When I first read the manuscript she produced, it prompted a reflection on the purpose of my life, and I was reminded of Justice V.R. Krishna Iyer's memorable words from *Bangalore Water Supply and Sewerage Board vs A. Rajappa and Others* in 1978: 'A life without a spiritual mission is a stillborn life.' I am glad to say mine has not been a still born life.

Isha Banerji, my editor at HarperCollins India, who is, surprisingly, almost sixty years younger than me. She insisted that I sit at my desk and bring this book to the finish line. It had been lying in the can for seven years; it was Isha who lit the final spark to complete it. I was amazed at our ability to communicate so easily despite the generational gap, in a world that has otherwise changed profoundly.

Kanishka Gupta, my agent from an ancient time, who wisely refused my repeated demands over the years to cancel the book contract. 'I will return the money,' I would tell him. I did not feel I wanted to write it. My life was already an open book—was there any need to put it to paper? I believed then that my words could not keep pace with my thoughts and actions, nor evolve with the changing patterns of my life or of the world around me. I am glad he persisted.

To Lawyers Collective, the organization I co-founded with my fellow trustees in the 1980s, and to all those who worked for it, a big thank you. It was, at the time, a first-of-its-kind NGO, offering voluntary legal services to meet the needs of those living in 'undeserved want' as in Article 41 of the directive principles—those for whom the Constitution holds a very special place. When the organization became one of the first to be targeted by the present NDA government in 2016, it was the trustees of Lawyers Collective who stood by Anand and me, forming a barrier against authoritarianism. Mihir Desai, Sanober Keshwar, Scharada Dubey, Firdous Abdul Moosa, Asmita Basu and Norma Alvares ensured we did not fall.

To the lawyers who represented us in the Supreme Court of India, Abhishek Manu Singhvi and other senior members of the bar, and to the young lawyers who turned out in large numbers in solidarity when orders were passed to investigate us, my thanks.

To Aspi Chinoy, who represented Lawyers Collective, the organization owes its continued work. And to Amit Desai, who continues to advise us to this day, and invariably tops his advice with several doses of gossip, we owe our gratitude.

To Rahul Karmarkar and Advait, the young lawyers who assisted us in court, I say: you are learning your law at my expense! Incidentally, Rahul is the grandson of a contemporary of mine; his grandfather, P.D. Karmarkar, a leading labour lawyer in Bombay, would, I am sure, be proud to know that Rahul stands with us.

Aditya Balasubramanian, who went through the manuscript, offered his comments and gave me confidence in a way only a historian, with a long-term perspective, can. I must also remember my late law school professor, Murli Bhandari, who, decades ago, tried—unsuccessfully—to ensure that I was not thrown out of Government Law college Bombay for want of attendance. He pleaded with the principal not to expel me, but the principal did not relent. We remained friends throughout our lives. Sunanda Bhandari, his late wife, remained an inspirational figure for the rest of her short life, displaying the kind of boldness required in the legal profession that only a woman can bring. Funnily enough, I later joined Siddharth College of Law, an institution founded by Dr Ambedkar, and secured a first class that year. He went back to the principal and told him, 'You missed out on a first-class student!' The moral of the story is that one does not learn the law in law school. I was very proud when Murli Bhandari's granddaughter, Shreya Sangal, came to me for her first internship.

I met Mohan Katarki when he was Bhandari's junior, and we stayed friends over the years. Our intense discussions on law, in chambers next door to each other, have always made me very happy, not least because I invariably get the better of him in the end. Without those exchanges, I would not be able to present a robust argument in court.

The women I represented—Mary Roy, Githa Hariharan, Vandana Shiva, Rupan Deol Bajaj, Ms X, Olga Tellis, Hasina Khan of Bebaak Collective and Ela Bhatt of SEWA—changed my life, as I hope I helped change theirs.

To the many women facing domestic violence who came to me, fleeing violent homes and abusive husbands, I owe so much; their stories helped me mould the Protection of Women from Domestic Violence Act, 2005.

To Justice V.R. Krishna Iyer and Justice P.N. Bhagwati, who admired me not so much for my legal knowledge as for my absence of sycophancy towards judges in general. I learned a great deal from the challenges they threw at me.

To Bindu Ammini, the first Dalit woman to climb the Sabarimala temple and perform darshan, I owe the inspiration to argue the Sabarimala case. It was worth it, even though she and Kanaka Durga were the only two women who succeeded. In response, the temple priests performed a shuddhikaran ceremony on the ground that 'untouchable' women had entered the shrine. It is that very judgment which is now under review.

To all those who worked on *The Lawyers*, the print edition of one of the earliest magazines on law and social justice, which began publication in Mumbai in 1986: In its first editorial, it declared that the purpose of the magazine was to 'break the silence around the judiciary and banish the fear of contempt of court'. As part of that mission, we published satire by our in-house satirist, Raju Z. Morey, and carried an anonymous column, 'Adalat Antics', which some called gossip, but which I preferred to think of as alternative news. No one sued us for defamation, for all that we published was true, except on one occasion when I received a notice from Soli Sorabjee stating I would be sued for contempt. I replied, 'But you are not the court; you are the Attorney General of India.' That was the end of the matter. To all those who helped bring out *The Lawyers*, my heartfelt thanks.

At the *Lawyers*, we were among the first to introduce humour and satire into legal journalism. Years later, in 2018, we went digital with The Leaflet. I have often been asked: How does one even begin a new venture at the age of seventy-nine? I am always surprised by this question. We are still around—a digital publication in the legal profession that focuses on the critical analysis of current judgments. To all our editors and legal journalists, past and present—Anshkanta Chakravarti (founding editor), Ramesh Menon, Venkatesh, Aayas Parry, Vineet Bhalla, Gurusimran Bakshi, Sushovan Patnaik, Ajitesh Singh and many other authors who have devoted their time and energy to keeping it going as a labour of love—I extend my thanks. The Leaflet means a great deal to me; it remains, in my view, a steady stream of resistance in the legal profession, keeping the law vibrant and responsive.

Why is legal journalism so important to me that I see it as a natural extension of my work in court? Because I believe that all professionals, like journalists, must be able to communicate with the public whom they serve. Law cannot remain within the confines of the courtroom; it must be taken to the people in language they can understand, freed from the coded incantations of 'whereas', 'notwithstanding' and 'without prejudice' of the legal profession. For me, there has never been any barrier between my work in court and my legal journalism. Both represent a stream of resistance within a democratized framework, without which the law cannot correct itself.

To my friend Dr Kalpana Swaminathan, an eminent paediatric surgeon, writer and fellow traveller, who has taught me new ways of seeing, and with whom I discuss many of my intellectual and moral dilemmas: she keeps me well with an energy-balanced diet, holding illness at bay for as long as possible.

To all the staff of our chambers and the Lawyers Collective—Usha Verma, Jagdish, Lalit Mohan, Sudha Prakash Assim, Gyan Prakash and Bharat Beriya—who keep the chambers running, my warm thanks.

And, finally, to my many unnamed juniors who uphold the tradition of ethical legal practice—may that tradition endure.

NOTES

1: Speaking for Myself

1. *Union Carbide Corporation Etc. vs Union of India* (1991), available at https://indiankanoon.org/doc/27098883/.
2. The *Olga Tellis vs Bombay Municipal Corporation* (1985).
3. See the chapter 'Bodily Integrity' for further details.

2: Democratic Lawyering

1. *ADM Jabalpur vs Shivkant Shukla etc* (1976), available at https://indiankanoon.org/doc/1735815/.
2. *Bombay Hawkers' Union vs Bombay Municipal Corporation*, AIR 1985 SC 1206.
3. *Olga Tellis vs Bombay Municipal Corporation*, AIR 1986 SC 180.
4. *Olga Tellis and Ors vs Bombay Municipal Corporation and Ors. etc on 10 July 1985*, Indian Kanoon, https://indiankanoon.org/doc/709776/.
5. *Self-Employed Women's Association & Ors vs Municipal Corporation of Ahmedabad & Ors,* Civil Miscellaneous Petition No. 32061(1986): Writ Petition 89(1982).

6. *Constituent Assembly Debates*, vol. 11.
7. Upendra Baxi, 'Taking Suffering Seriously: Social Action Litigation in the Supreme Court of India', *Third World Legal Studies*, Vol. 4, Article 6, http://scholar.valpo.edu/twls/vol4/iss1/6.
8. It was done at the request of the National Commission for Women, then led by Chairperson Dr V. Mohini Giri.
9. Indira Jaising, 'Concern for the Dead, Condemnation for the Living', *Economic and Political Weekly* 49:30 (2014), 34–38.
10. Dr B.R. Ambedkar, *Castes in India: Their Mechanism, Genesis and Development*, Anthropology Seminar of Dr A.A. Goldenweiser, Columbia University, New York, 9 May 1916.
    Dr B.R. Ambedkar, Annihilation of Caste, edited and annotated by S. Anand (Gurugram: Penguin Random House India), p. 16.
11. This exception appears as Exception 2 appended to Section 375 of the Indian Penal Code, 1860, as the statutory definition of the offence of rape in India. It has been retained in the Bharatiya Nyaya Sanhita 2024 as Exception 2 to Section 63.
12. For details, see the next chapter 'Secular Lawyering'.

3: Secular Lawyering

1. Article 13(1): All laws in force in the territory of India immediately before the commencement of this Constitution, in so far as they are inconsistent with the provisions of this Part, shall, to the extent of such inconsistency, be void.
2. The State shall not make any law which takes away or abridges the rights conferred by this Part and any law made in contravention of this clause shall, to the extent of the contravention, be void.
3. In this article, unless the context otherwise requires—

(a) 'law' includes any Ordinance, order, bye-law, rule, regulation, notification, custom or usage having in the territory of India the force of law;
(b) 'laws in force' includes laws passed or made by a Legislature or other competent authority in the territory of India before the commencement of this Constitution and not previously repealed, notwithstanding that any such law or any part thereof may not be then in operation either at all or in particular areas.
2. Article 15(1) The State shall not discriminate against any citizen on grounds only of religion, race, caste, sex, place of birth or any of them.
The State of Bombay vs Narasu Appa Mali, AIR 1952 Bom 84 (Bombay High Court, 24 July 1951), available at https://indiankanoon.org/doc/54613/.

4. Freedom of conscience and free profession, practice and propagation of religion:
25(1) Subject to public order, morality and health and to the other provisions of this Part, all persons are equally entitled to freedom of conscience and the right freely to profess, practise and propagate religion.
(2) Nothing in this article shall affect the operation of any existing law or prevent the State from making any law—
(a) regulating or restricting any economic, financial, political or other secular activity which may be associated with religious practice;
(b) providing for social welfare and reform or the throwing open of Hindu religious institutions of a public character to all classes and sections of Hindus.
Explanation I: The wearing and carrying of kirpans shall be deemed to be included in the profession of the Sikh religion.
Explanation II: In sub-clause (b) of clause (2), the reference to Hindus shall be construed as including a reference to

persons professing the Sikh, Jain or Buddhist religion, and the reference to Hindu religious institutions shall be construed accordingly.

5. See Article 13 of the Constitution of India.
6. Abolition of Untouchability—
   Article 17: 'Untouchability' is abolished and its practice in any form is forbidden. The enforcement of any disability arising out of 'Untouchability' shall be an offence punishable in accordance with law. https://indiankanoon.org/doc/1987997/
7. 'Article 25: Constitution of India', available at https://indiankanoon.org/doc/631708/.
8. 'Article 14: Constitution of India', available at https://indiankanoon.org/doc/367586/.
9. 'Article 15: Constitution of India', available at https://indiankanoon.org/doc/609295/.
10. Uniform Civil Code for Citizens
11. Article 44. The State shall endeavour to secure for the citizens a uniform civil code throughout the territory of India.
12. Entry 5 of List III (the Concurrent List) in the Seventh Schedule of the Indian Constitution gives both the Parliament and State legislatures the power to make laws on personal matters such as marriage, divorce, adoption, succession and joint family—areas traditionally governed by personal or customary law.
13. Bebaak Collective (meaning Voices of the Fearless) was founded in 2013 as an informal association of autonomous grassroots activists in 2013 advocating for the rights of women marginalized by religion, including Muslim women. The collective works to raise awareness, campaign against injustice and raise funds for victims of communal hate and marginalization. Its focus is on exposing the structural violence against women that emerges from everyday violence around caste, class, religion and on emphasizing the importance of collective struggle.

It has campaigned on several critical issues, including the abolition of triple talaq, the ban on beef and vigilante violence by gau rakshaks (cow vigilantes). It also works to raise media awareness on these matters. The group organizes conferences, collective discussions and reading circles to engage with historical and contemporary issues and translate them into action.

14. *Shayara Bano vs Union of India* (2017), available at https://indiankanoon.org/doc/115701246/.
15. The Delhi High Court judgment (*Harvinder Kaur vs Harmander Singh Choudhury* [1976], on restitution of conjugal rights), observed that constitutional law is like 'a bull in a china shop'—a belief that family law is too delicate, too sacrosanct, to be disrupted. That image has stayed with me. Decisions like these still stand as the law of the land. The Shayara Bano case did not succeed in dismantling them, but at least it left a dent.
16. *The State of Bombay vs Narasu Appa Mali* (1951), available at https://indiankanoon.org/doc/54613/?type=print.
17. Ibid.
18. Ibid.
19. Ibid.
20. Ibid.
21. 'Section 3 in The Muslim Women (Protection of Rights on Divorce) Act, 1986', available at https://indiankanoon.org/doc/976981/.
22. 'Sabarimala temple: India court questions women entry ban', BBC News, 11 January 2016, available at https://www.bbc.com/news/world-south-asia-35278562.
23. 'Article 25 in Constitution of India', available at https://indiankanoon.org/doc/631708/.
24. *Indian Young Lawyers Association vs The State of Kerala* (2018), available at https://indiankanoon.org/doc/163639357/.
25. Ibid.

26. Indira Jaising, 'The Ghost of Narsu Appa Mali Is Stalking the Supreme Court of India', *Lawyers Collective*, 28 May 2018.
27. *Indian Young Lawyers Association vs The State of Kerala.*
28. 'Communist govts. acquiring Hindu temples for revenue: Former SC judge', *The Hindu*, 28 August 2022, https://www.thehindu.com/news/national/kerala/communist-govts-acquiring-hindu-temples-for-revenue-former-sc-judge/article65823843.ece
29. 'Section 6 in The Hindu Minority and Guardianship Act, 1956', available at https://indiankanoon.org/doc/39958047/.
30. *Ms. Githa Hariharan & Anr vs Reserve Bank of India & Anr* (1999), available at https://indiankanoon.org/doc/1241462/.
31. *Mary Roy and Ors. vs State of Kerala and Ors* (1986), 2 SCC 209.
32. A category of states formed from former princely states or unions of such states that had acceded to India, typically led by former rulers as the head of the constituent states. In July 1949, the former State of Travancore merged with the former State of Cochin to create the State of Travancore–Cochin, later classified as a Part B state under the Constitution. The States Reorganisation Act and the Constitution (Seventh Amendment) Act, 1956, did away with this distinction.
33. Also known as agiaries: a circular, raised structure built by Zoroastrians for excarnation.
34. *Goolrokh M. Gupta vs Burjor Pardiwala & Ors* (2012), SCA No. 449/2010.
35. Madhya Pradesh Dharma Swatantraya Adhiniyam (1968).
36. Orissa Freedom of Religion Act, 1967.
37. *Reverend Stanislaus vs State of Madhya Pradesh & Ors on 17 January 1977, 977 SCR (2) 611.*
38. Law Commission of India Consultation Paper on Reform of Family Law, 31 August 2018, available at https://archive.pib.gov.in/documents/rlink/2018/aug/p201883101.pdf.

4: Bodily Integrity

1. *Vishaka and Others vs State of Rajasthan* (1997), available at https://indiankanoon.org/doc/1031794/.
2. *Mrs Rupan Deol Bajaj & Anr vs Kanwar Pal Singh Gill & Anr on 12 October 1995*, available at https://indiankanoon.org/doc/579822/.
3. The record tells another story. Several cases still pending point to 'disappearances' from that period, to deaths written off as part of a so-called 'encounter' strategy carried out in utter disregard of the law.
4. See John Burns, 'Ex-Policeman's Jail Term Hailed by Women in India', *The New York Times*, 12 August 1996, available at https://www.nytimes.com/1996/08/12/world/ex-policeman-s-jail-term-hailed-by-women-in-india.html.
5. 'A Policy of Impunity in Punjab, India: I. Summary', Human Rights Watch, available at https://www.hrw.org/reports/2007/india1007/1.htm.
6. Dhananjay Mahapatra, 'Gwalior additional judge says she was sexually harassed by HC judge, quits', *Times of India*, 4 August 2013, available at https://timesofindia.indiatimes.com/india/gwalior-additional-judge-says-she-was-sexually-harassed-by-hc-judge-quits/articleshow/39569700.cms.
7. *Additional District and Sessions Judge 'X' vs Registrar General, High Court of Madhya Pradesh and Others* (2014), available at https://api.sci.gov.in/jonew/courtnic/rop/2014/28283/rop_188247.pdf.
8. It is a different matter that he never sat in court after that, but though held guilty of corruption, he was never removed as a judge. He retired and drew his pension for life.

5: The Lost Years

1. 'Letter From Sally Yates', *New York Times*, 30 January 2017, https://www.nytimes.com/interactive/2017/01/30/us/document-Letter-From -Sally-Yates.html
2. The Foreign Contribution (Regulation) Act, 2010.
3. 'Court turns down Gujarat Police, will hear Sanjiv Bhatt's request for bail', NDTV, 7 October 2011, available at https://www.ndtv.com/india-news/court-turns-down-gujarat-police-will-hear-sanjiv-bhatts-request-for-bail-565248.

6: Who Is a Citizen?

1. 'Rights of citizenship of certain persons who have migrated to India from Pakistan', Constitution of India, available at https://www.constitutionofindia.net/articles/article-6-rights-of-citizenship-of-certain-persons-who-have-migrated-to-india-from-pakistan/.
2. 'Article 7 in Constitution of India', available at https://indiankanoon.org/doc/735354/.
3. Ibid.
4. The Influx from West Pakistan (Control) Ordinance, 1948 No. XVII of 1948, 19 July 1948, available at https://partitiondisplacements.com/wp-content/uploads/The-Influx-from-West-Pakistan-Control-Ordinance-1948.pdf.
5. N. Gopalaswami Ayyangar, Constituent Assembly Debates, Vol. 9, 12 August 1949, 9.117.121, available at https://www.constitutionofindia.net/debates/12-aug-1949/.
6. *Annual Report: 1952–53 of the Ministry of External Affairs*, 1 January 1952.
7. *T.M.A. Pai Foundation vs State of Karnataka* (2002).

8. Ibad Mushtaq, 'What does "citizenship" mean in India', The Leaflet, 20 April 2022, available at https://theleaflet.in/governance-and-policy/what-does-citizenship-mean-in-india.
9. 'Writ Petition (C) No 274 of 2009', Re: Section 6A of the Citizenship Act 1955, available at https://api.sci.gov.in/supremecourt/2009/16113/16113_2009_1_1501_56604_Judgement_17-Oct-2024.pdf.
10. *Constitutional Assembly Debates*, 12 August 1949, 9.111.32.

7: The Constitution Is My Home

1. *Indian Young Lawyers Association vs the State of Kerala* (2018).
2. Directive Principles of State Policy (DPSPs) are guidelines for the Indian government to establish social and economic justice within the country
3. 'Ram is the foundation of India. Ram is the idea of India, Ram is the law of India.' Quoted in Narendra Modi, 'Narendra Modi's Ayodhya speech: Ram is not fire, Ram is energy. Ram is not a dispute, Ram is a solution. Ram is not just ours, Ram belongs to everyone', *The Indian Express*, 23 January 2024, available at https://indianexpress.com/article/opinion/columns/ayodhya-ram-mandir-inauguration-lord-ram-narendra-modi-ram-setu-ramlalla-9122567/.
4. 'Ordinarily, Hindutva is understood as a way of life or a state of mind and it is not to be equated with or understood as religious Hindu fundamentalism.' *Ramesh Yeshwant Prabhoo vs Prabhakar Kashinath Kunte*, (1996) AIR 1113 (SC).
5. C.O. 273, Presidential Order (6th August 2019).
6. The Constitution (One Hundred and Third Amendment) Act, 2019, Act No. 28 of 2019, Date of Assent: 12th January 2019.
7. It can, however, be argued that the citizenship act is a part of the Constitutional framework, just as the Representation of People Act, 1951, is considered an addition to Article 324.

8. 1976 AIR 1207
9. Arvind Narrain, *India's Undeclared Emergency: Constitutionalism and the Politics of Resistance* (New Delhi: Westland), 2021.
10. Neelam Pandey and Shanker Arnimesh, 'RSS in Modi govt in numbers — 3 of 4 ministers are rooted in the Sangh.' The Print, 27 January 2020, available at https://theprint.in/politics/rss-in-modi-govt-in-numbers-3-of-4-ministers-are-rooted-in-the-sangh/353745/.
11. 'Controversially unapologetic: Tathagata Roy's most provoking statements', *Indian Express,* 21 February 2019. https://indianexpress.com/article/india/governor-tathagata-roy-most-controversial-statements-5594182/
12. *Supreme Court Advocates-on-Record -Association vs Union of India* (2015), available at https://indiankanoon.org/doc/66970168/.
13. *Association For Democratics Reforms vs Union ofIndia* (2024), INSC 113, available at https://indiankanoon.org/doc/121499464/.
14. 'BBC SPECIAL: Narendra Modi is a model, a hero: Chief Justice of Patna High Court', BBC Hindi, 14 August 2018, available at https://www.bbc.com/hindi/india-45180308.
15. Sudhir Krishnaswamy and Advay Vora, 'Master of the Roster: Securing Process Legitimacy of the Supreme Court', SC Observer, 13 September 2024, available at https://www.scobserver.in/75-years-of-sc/master-of-the-roster-securing-process-legitimacy-of-the-supreme-court/.
16. Criminal Appeal Nos. 1184–85 of 2023 (Arising out of SLP (Crl.) Nos. 11072–73/2022).
17. '"Brain is more dangerous, direct involvement is not necessary", SC during hearing in Prof G.N. Saibaba's case', ET LegalWorld.com, 17 October 2022, available at https://legal.economictimes.indiatimes.com/news/industry/brain-is-more-dangerous-direct-

involvement-is-not-necessary-sc-during-hearing-in-prof-g-n-saibaba-case/94906905.

18. Section 124A: Sedition.
19. The rule of law on which a judicial decision is based.
20. 1962 INSC 200.
21. On 5 October 2020, Siddique Kappan, a Muslim journalist, was arrested on his way to Hathras district in Uttar Pradesh. He had set out to report on the rape and death of a young Dalit woman that had triggered nationwide protests. He was reportedly held incommunicado for two days. On 7 October, state authorities revealed that he was being investigated for a wide sweep of offences: sedition (Section 124A IPC); 'promoting enmity between different groups on grounds of religion, race, place of birth, residence, language, etc' (Section 153A, IPC); 'deliberate and malicious acts, intended to outrage religious feelings of any class by insulting its religion or religious beliefs' (Section 295A, IPC); 'knowingly holding property derived or obtained from the commission of a terrorist act' (Section 14 (UAPA); 'raising funds for terrorist acts' (Section 17, UAPA); 'destroying digital evidence' (Section 65, Information Technology Act); and 'breach of confidentiality and privacy' (Section 72, Information Technology Act).
22. Sunil Khilnani, *The Idea of India* (New York: Farrar, Straus, Giroux), 1997.
23. 'Ram Mandir Pran Pratistha | 'Ram Is Faith, Foundation, Idea of India, Says PM Modi In Fervent Speech', Mint, available at https://www.youtube.com/watch?v=AHTZir7xCmQ.
24. M.K. Gandhi, *Young India*, 22 October 1919, p. 1, in *Collected Works of Mahatma Gandhi*, Vol. 15 (Publications Division, Government of India).

8: Doing Justice

1. Justice K. Chandru (Retd.), 'The silver maces and panic buttons: The impeachment story of Justice V. Ramaswami', The Leaflet, 22 June 2025, available at https://theleaflet.in/judicial-accountability/the-silver-maces-and-panic-buttons-the-impeachment-story-of-justice-v-ramaswami.
2. I was present during the proceedings of the court. This order was also cited by Justices Arun Misra and Khehar in the judgment of the Ms X case in the High Court of Madhya Pradesh.
3. Suchitra Kalyan Mohanty, 'Senior advocates urge CJI to direct CBI action against Allahabad HC judge for hate speech at VHP event', *The New Indian Express*, 18 January 2025, available at https://www.newindianexpress.com/nation/2025/Jan/17/senior-advocates-urge-cji-to-direct-cbi-action-against-allahabad-hc-judge-for-hate-speech-at-vhp-event.

9: The Rule of Law

1. The Code of Hammurabi, a Babylonian collection of 282 legal edicts from around 1750 BCE, is one of the earliest recorded legal codes.
2. Fernanda Pirie, *The Rule of Laws: A 4,000-year Quest to Order the World* (London: Profile Books), 2021, p. 70.
3. 'Kangana Ranaut slams Indira Jaising for seeking pardon for rapists, says "such women give birth to monsters"' *Hindustan Times*, 30 August 2020, available at https://www.hindustantimes.com/bollywood/kangana-ranaut-slams-indira-jaising-for-seeking-pardon-for-rapists-says-such-women-give-birth-to-monsters/story-vanPtWVnWGrcfmQXU0H7IM.html.

ABOUT THE AUTHORS

Indira Jaising is a pioneering lawyer and human rights activist known for her work on gender justice, labour rights and constitutional freedoms in India. A senior advocate at the Supreme Court, she became the first woman to serve as Additional Solicitor General of the country (2009–14). She also served as a member of the United Nations Committee on the Elimination of Discrimination against Women (2009–12) and was instrumental in drafting the Protection of Women from Domestic Violence Act, 2005.

Jaising is a co-founder of the Lawyers Collective, an organization that has played a major role in advancing public interest litigation and rights-based advocacy in India, and a co-founder of The Leaflet, an independent digital platform for critical analysis of legal issues. She was awarded the Padma Shri in 2005. In 2018, *Fortune* magazine named her one of the World's 50 Greatest Leaders.

Ritu Menon is a feminist publisher and writer. She is the co-founder of Kali for Women and the founder of Women Unlimited. Among her published books are *Borders & Boundaries: Women in India's Partition*; *Out of Line: A Literary and Political Biography of Nayantara Sahgal*; *Zohra!: A Biography in Four Acts*; *Address Book: A Publishing Memoir in the Time of COVID*; *Loitering with Intent: Diary of a Happy Traveller*; and *India on Their Minds: 8 Women, 8 Ideas of India*. She was awarded the Padma Shri in 2011.

HarperCollins *Publishers* India

At HarperCollins India, we believe in telling the best stories and finding the widest readership for our books in every format possible. We started publishing in 1992; a great deal has changed since then, but what has remained constant is the passion with which our authors write their books, the love with which readers receive them, and the sheer joy and excitement that we as publishers feel in being a part of the publishing process.

Over the years, we've had the pleasure of publishing some of the finest writing from the subcontinent and around the world, including several award-winning titles and some of the biggest bestsellers in India's publishing history. But nothing has meant more to us than the fact that millions of people have read the books we published, and that somewhere, a book of ours might have made a difference.

As we look to the future, we go back to that one word—a word which has been a driving force for us all these years.

Read.

Harper Collins
Harper Sport
HARPER FICTION
HARPER NON-FICTION
हार्पर हिन्दी

HARPER LEARNING
HARPER VANTAGE
HCCB HARPERCOLLINS CHILDREN'S BOOKS
4th
HARPER PERENNIAL

HARPER DESIGN
BOOKTOPUS
HARPER BUSINESS